We owe Steve Chalke a great deal for his perseverance with faithworks. Now we discover what motivates him: a combination of Christian faith and works. As St. John of the Cross said: 'Mission is putting love where love is not.' This book is full of ideas. It should prompt us all to examine the effectiveness of the way local churches are organized.

—The Most Reverend and Right Honourable
Dr. John Sentamu, Archbishop of York

Everything that Steve Chalke writes is insightful and cutting-edge and this book is no exception. Here he argues in favor of a Church that thinks and acts in ways that actualize the kind of social relevancy that makes the Kingdom of God visible and reasonable in a secular society.

—Tony Campolo, Ph.D. Eastern University

Warm, hopeful, hands-on help, written from a fellow traveler and practitioner and not an armchair theorist. Full of passion and energy. Some books about the church depress me. This impressed and inspired me. Buy it.

—Jeff Lucas, Author, Speaker, and Broadcaster

Steve Chalke is one of the clearest and most passionate voices we have for calling the church to be what we are supposed to be. In his last book, he reveals the 'lost message of Jesus' and beckons us back to our movement's founder. In this new book, Steve Chalke shows how the church can actually be 'intelligent,' at a time when many skeptics find that hard to believe. The Intelligent Church is a primer for churches seeking to be lovers of justice, lovers of truth, and a voice of reason in a society that often lacks all three. He describes the values, principles and theology that offer an intelligent and authentic response to people searching for spiritual insight. This is a timely and much needed book.

—Jim Wallis, author of *God's Politics*

INTELLIGENT
CHURCH

INTELLIGENT
CHURCH

STEVE CHALKE
AND ANTHONY WATKIS

ZONDERVAN™

GRAND RAPIDS, MICHIGAN 49530 USA

ZONDERVAN.COM/
AUTHORTRACKER

ZONDERVAN™

Intelligent Church
Copyright © 2006 by Steve Chalke

Requests for information should be addressed to:

Zondervan, *Grand Rapids, Michigan 49530*

Library of Congress Cataloging-in-Publication Data

Chalke, Steve.
      Intelligent church : a journey towards Christ-centred community /
         Steve Chalke and Anthony Watkis.— 1st ed.
      p. cm.
      ISBN-13: 978-0-310-24884-2
      ISBN-10: 0-310-24884-1
      1. Mission of the church. 2. Church. I. Watkis, Anthony. II. Title.
BV601.8.C43 2006
270.8'3—dc22

                                     2006001097
        CIP

Steve Chalke and Anthony Watkis assert the moral right to be identified as the authors of this work.

The website addresses recommended throughout this book are offered as a resource to you. These websites are not intended in any way to be or imply an endorsement on the part of Zondervan, nor do we vouch for their content for the life of this book.

Interior design by Mark Sheeres

Printed in the United Kingdom

06 07 08 09 10 11 12 • 10 9 8 7 6 5 4 3 2 1

CONTENTS

O   O   O

FOREWORD

BRIAN D. MCLAREN

O   O   O

For those who have never read a book or heard a lecture by Steve Chalke, this is a great place to start. For starters, in *Intelligent Church* you'll get a feel for Steve's intelligence, which is formidable because Steve's active and creative mind is always reading, always questioning, always wondering, always penetrating. But you'll be even more struck by how his intelligence, along with that of his absolutely brilliant coauthor, Anthony Watkis, is linked to his passion, how his head works with his heart. Together, their intelligence, like the intelligent church of which they speak, is about wisdom harnessed for service, understanding focused in love.

In these pages you'll also be introduced to Steve's skill as a storyteller. He's one of the best. Like another storyteller who walked this earth about 2000 years ago, Steve's stories carry a meaning that stays with you and just might change your life.

And you'll also be introduced to Steve's deep faith. Steve and I share a friendship with a number of other Christian leaders around the world who have gained a reputation for being unconventional, sometimes controversial. But anyone who is upset with how Steve might cross a theological 'i' or dot a theological 't' (the mistake was intentional) will see in these pages how Steve is truly a Jesus-man, dedicated to following Jesus in both word and deed. Steve wants to teach what Jesus taught in the manner Jesus taught it, and he wants to do what Jesus did too. No, I'm not aware of him walking on water or multiplying loaves and fishes or raising the dead. But I know he has traveled across the world's oceans to share the good news of

Jesus, and I know he is constantly raising funds and personnel so that those in need can be fed and cared for, and I know that he leads people into needy neighborhoods where there is too much death in order to bring hope and life.

Steve is an example to me of integral mission. He understands, as you'll better understand through this book, that the good news of Jesus encompasses and integrates all of life—how we treat a person of a different race, religion, or sexual orientation, how we think about politics or the environment, how we face our intellectual doubts, how we structure our church so that outsiders can become insiders.

And he is also an example to me of reflective or contemplative activism. His chapters on intelligence and dependence show how thought and prayer—and prayerful thought and thoughtful prayer—must undergird all we do. But the activism and energy that pulsate on every page remind us that Steve's life hasn't been about forming committees to study problems from a distance so that reports could be written. No, Steve has been about getting out on the streets and making a difference—and bringing others along with him for the adventure.

So, in these pages you'll be exposed to some of the best ideas of an amazing leader whom I feel deeply privileged to know and from whom I have learned much. But Steve's not just interested in us learning a lot. He's interested in us getting out on the streets and making a difference. That's why he has written about the church.

Steve and Anthony know, as many of us do, that too often our churches have become human warehouses, where people are gathered and stored so that they can be delivered after death to heaven with minimum loss, spoilage, rust, rot, or breakage. These air-conditioned warehouses are equipped with every comfort—from padded seats to a kind of religious muzak—so that those who enter will be happy and never want to leave until they are shipped to their final destination.

But like salt that has gotten too comfortable living in a saltshaker, we need to be shaken up and shaken out of our religious boxes. So our churches need to rediscover their missional calling and move from being defensive and closed to outgoing and open.

Those of us who are pastors or committed members of churches know that this kind of inside-out transformation is not easy. Resistance is widespread and strong for a whole host of reasons. Those of us who see that the status quo is unacceptable sometimes feel that we're beating our heads against a church wall, and the wall is holding firm. Sometimes, frankly, it's discouraging.

That's where Steve Chalke and Anthony Watkis come in. Their gift of encouragement helps me feel that more and more of those walls can come down if we just don't give up. And I know they're right.

So enjoy this book, and let's be collaborators with Steve and Anthony in putting it into practice, wherever we are. This world needs an explosion of churches that are passionately involved in what Steve calls faithworks.

— Brian McLaren, Washington, DC

INTRODUCTION:
CHALLENGE OF THE AGES

○ ○ ○

Albert Einstein once commented that 'the kind of thinking
that will solve the world's problems will be of a different order
to the kind of thinking that created those problems in the first
place.' At the beginning of the third millennium the church in
the West needs a different order of thinking. Our task must be
to consider what we believe to be the nonnegotiables of our
faith and, in the light of this understanding of God's mission
and purpose for his people, reimagine our purpose and mission,
allowing them to shape the way we do church for the twenty-
first century. To put it in technical language, our theology (our
understanding of God) must unpack itself through our missiology (our understanding of mission) which must shape our
ecclesiology (our understanding of church).

The challenge of the ages is set before us all. What will be
our epitaph? Will we be the generation that began to rebuild
the church in the West, or will we simply preside over its further demise? My very great hope is that we will rise to the
challenge. Not in order to preserve a crumbling institution the
way the National Trust restores old castles and stately homes
in the UK—the interesting relics of a bygone age, historically
important but of little modern relevance—but instead to build
Christ's church anew that we might bring genuinely good news
to God's world.

Much has been said of late about the concept of 'emerging
church'—the phrase itself speaks the language of change and
transition. But the truth is, of course, that the church has been
emerging for two thousand years. We have constantly been in

transition — each generation is called to reinvent or rediscover what it is to model accessible and authentic church within its surrounding culture. The problem is that of late we have seen more churches closing (in the sense of both dying communities and redundant buildings) than ever before. In this age more than any that preceded it, we need to ask what an intelligent and biblical response to our culture looks like. What is an intelligent church?

In the coming pages we will consider some of the hallmarks that I believe our churches should bear — those of authentic Christian spirituality. The method will be simple: in each chapter we will consider the relationship between theology, missiology and ecclesiology.

The content of too many books ends up as a distant memory for the busy practitioner. We end up doing the same with what we have read as what we often do with what the preacher has said. We hear it all and agree with much of it but simply don't know how to apply it to our lives. Though we may resoundingly shout 'Yes' with our hearts, our heads shout 'But how?' How do we make this work? How do we help the people in our congregation grasp this?

These are important questions, and for that reason, every chapter of this book ends with a brief section called 'Yes, But How?' In it, you'll find five practical ideas on how to move from reading it to doing it and being it. The sections are deliberately brief so that you can get a handle on what you have read and do something with it. They are designed to start your thinking on how to translate the principles of this book into practice. They are not prescriptive. They are simply a selection of ideas to get you started or to keep you going, whichever best fits your situation. And, if you need to get help with any of the ideas, remember you can contact Faithworks for more information and support at info@faithworks.info or through our Web site, www.faithworks.info.

CHAPTER 1

INTELLIGENT
CHURCH

I had a strange experience recently. I was at a weekend retreat in the Wiltshire countryside with some of the leadership team of my church. At lunchtime on Saturday a few of us ventured to the supermarket in the nearest town to buy food. As we walked up to the doors of the shop, we noticed a few people standing outside the building with a banner announcing Saint Luke's Church. Thinking that this was part of the church's mission to the local community, we decided to stop for a chat and to offer some encouragement. Incredibly, though, as we approached, a man in clerical dress started shaking a collection tin in our faces. He was, it seems, of the belief that we (and, presumably, the rest of those out shopping for groceries) should make a donation to Saint Luke's organ refurbishment fund. We stopped and talked, but however hard we tried to change the conversation, they were only interested in discussing keyboards, pedals and pipes. As we wandered off I was overcome by the sad realisation that the only message the shoppers heard from the church that day was, 'We're broke. Please save us!'

This story is a modern-day parable. I can almost hear it — told with style — on the lips of Jesus. It triggers me to consider again the purpose of the church. Have we concentrated our efforts in the right place? Are we trying so hard to save ourselves that we've forgotten what we are really here to do? Who are we? Why do we exist? How do we develop an intelligent response to the communities in which we find ourselves living?

REDEFINITION

Intelligent churches in the twenty-first century will take many different forms, but window dressing is not our concern here. Rather, the task ahead is to nail down what it means to *be* church — to discern what core values, principles, and theology should be the hallmarks of our churches. We will determine not what shape churches should take as much as from what substance they should be formed.

A former archbishop of Canterbury, William Temple, prophetically warned, 'If a man's concept of God is at error, the more fundamentally committed he is to it, the more damage he will do.' With that in mind, we need to consider again the way in which we approach the task of being church by reflecting on who God is. What we believe about God fundamentally shapes our view of the church, and that, in turn, determines how we live out its mission. Our behaviour, both personally and communally, is simply an outworking of our beliefs.

It is critical that our generation redefine what the church has to say to the world, engaging with and critiquing our culture as many of the generations before us have engaged with theirs. But we will not recapture the success of the church of ages past simply by replicating their methods or even, to an extent, their message. As Franklin D. Roosevelt famously stated, 'Eternal truths will neither be true nor eternal unless they have fresh meaning for every new social situation.' We need an intelligent response to our society — by which I do not mean cerebral or intellectual, but rather wise, relevant, and authentic. We need churches that make sense of both the Bible and of conventional wisdom. We need Christians who know theology, culture, and the application of one to the other.

STATE OF THE CHURCH

At present it seems that no matter how you look at the situation of the church, something has gone wrong. The signs are not good. Every few months or so, the people who are interested in counting, calculating and forecasting confront us with a new bundle of depressing statistics about the church in the West. Church attendance figures, they tell us, are tumbling. Although by no means uniform across the denominations or the nations, the statistics for the Western church as a whole look, at best, grim.

Looking farther afield than the United Kingdom, it would be easy to conclude that matters are much better. The church in the United States is, on one level, thriving. The United States is home to some of the most enormous and influential churches on earth—some attracting tens of thousands of people each week. However, an increasing number of churches are finding their pews or chairs emptier with each passing Sunday.

While speaking at a conference run by the Southern Baptist denomination, addressing the nation's church planters, I congratulated them on their astonishing success. However, when I went out for a meal with a group of their national leaders, I was told that half of their churches had far fewer in their congregations than I had assumed. The average size of a Southern Baptist church, they informed me, was under fifty members—a marked decline when compared to the situation just a few years earlier. The symptoms of the fall of Christendom are, it seems, creeping up on the United States too. Though the media is keen to point to the power of America's religious right, a walk through most of the country's multicultural cities reveals a very different story.

Even weddings, funerals and christenings (previously the big three events that would draw people into church buildings) are becoming less commonly 'Christian'. People are often getting married and buried in secular, or at least secularized, ceremonies. The baptism of infants, too, is increasingly rare among nominally Christian families. And religious festivals (such as Good Friday and Easter), which in decades past were guaranteed pew fillers, now seldom attract more than a handful of unfamiliar faces. Christmas is the only Christian holiday that retains a semblance of theological imagery and attracts the casual believer to a church service—and even that is fading as Winterval, the secularized holiday, becomes increasingly prevalent.

But why should this be the case? Jesus still commands huge respect. I remember chatting with a friend over dinner shortly after he'd been invited to speak at Harvard University. He told me that he had asked the president of the university why he had been given such a wonderful opportunity. The president responded with an intriguing story. He explained that some months earlier he had gathered together a group of his senior faculty for a discussion day during which he had raised the subject of Jesus. The response was overwhelmingly positive. Jesus was described as wise, compassionate, generous, gracious, liberating and forgiving. But later that day, when he asked the same group of tutors their opinions of the church, they gave very different answers—judgemental, bigoted, self-righteous, censorious, finger-wagging and excluding. My friend had been invited to 'redress the balance'. But the president's words to him were stern: 'You've got a problem—a very big problem.'

SPIRITUAL HUNGER

The church is often tempted to lay the blame for our decline on the values of the culture in which we live. People nowadays, we say, aren't interested in church because they have been seduced by the corrupting influences of the age—the sex, the drugs, the rock and roll, the consumerism and the leisure—and have little concept of sin. But, while it is true that many of the trappings of Western culture are greatly distracting, this is no more true for us than it was for our counterparts living within the first-century Roman Empire—the years that saw the church grow from a clutch of people hiding in an upper room in Jerusalem into a movement that changed the world.

People within our post-Christian society are hungry for spiritual insight and direction. After his son's birth, the world-famous soccer star David Beckham somewhat obliquely commented, 'I've a definite sense of spirituality. I want Brooklyn to be christened, but I don't know into what religion yet.' Though they might not necessarily use familiar language to describe it, people are longing for meaning and purpose in their lives, acutely aware of their failings and inconsistencies—they are searching for God. References to spirituality are everywhere. Religion, albeit noninstitutional, is a boom market. People in our postmodern, post-Christian age are certainly not closed to matters spiritual; indeed, I believe they are as spiritually open and searching as any generation that preceded them.

A few years back I was frequently invited to speak to university students addressing the question, 'How can I believe in God in an age of science?' For a number of years it was without doubt the subject I was asked to address most often—so pressing was the question. But it's been so long since I was last booked to speak on this once hot potato that I've forgotten what I used to say. What was once a burning issue is now seen as irrelevant.

Today vast numbers of people have an intrinsic understanding of spirituality—they see it as part of everyday life. And yet fewer and fewer of them venture across the threshold of our church buildings. In spite of a deep, indeed growing, sense of spiritual awareness and genuine longing for God (whatever the conception of the divine), fewer people would consider visiting a church building than even a decade ago. Why?

Last year I was given the opportunity to run in the New York Marathon, and so I found myself on the eve of the race in Times Square with my wife, Cornelia. As we wandered around, dazzled by the bright lights of the gigantic billboards, we became aware of a group of eight or ten well-built, muscular men in their twenties and thirties, one of whom was shouting at the crowd and waving a big stick at them. Curious as to what was going on we rather gingerly drew closer to the group to hear what they were saying. As we did so, it became obvious that they were Christians and that they were engaged in some sort of street outreach. The man with the stick was pointing it at the passersby and shouting at the top of his voice about their 'iniquitous lives'. Every now and then he would turn to an even bigger man beside him (bearing a striking similarity to Mr. T from the old television series *The A-Team*) who was holding a huge Bible. The leader would order Mr. T to read a verse from the Scriptures.

'Give me that Deuteronomy 32:22,' he would shout.

'"For a fire has been kindled by my wrath, one that burns to the realm of death below. It will devour the earth and its harvests and set afire the foundations of the mountains,"' would come Mr. T's dutiful reply. Their message was clear to everyone in the square — God doesn't like you very much, and if you don't change your ways he's going to burn you.

I decided, much to Cornelia's embarrassment and fear, that I had to get involved. I walked into the centre of the group and interrupted the show to remind all who were gathered of God's overwhelming, unstoppable and undeserved love for them and all humanity. The crowd was growing all the time, and so, my confidence rising, I turned to Mr. T and ordered, 'Give me 1 John 4:9–10.' He didn't move a muscle. So I quoted it as best I could from memory. 'This is how God showed his love among us: He sent his one and only Son into the world that we might live through him. This is love: not that we loved

God, but that he loved us and sent his Son as an atoning sacrifice for our sins.'

All I could hear was my heart beating much louder than normal and a few of the onlookers who had started to snigger. The silence was broken when the group's leader pointed at Mr. T and boomed at me, 'He reads only what *I* tell him to read!'

We are not changed by moral exhortation but rather by being shown a different and better reality. The best starting point is always to affirm rather than condemn. The great sweep, the meta-narrative, of the Bible is of God's love for us, and communicating that message to our generation is our primary task—indeed to fail to do so is to fail to preach an authentic gospel. The task of the church is to be the irrefutable demonstration and proof of the fact that God is love. God's nature is revealed through his works. If the church is part of the work of God then its primary responsibility is to announce this truth. Donald English once called this the 'deep resonance of the biblical text'. When people are lost it does not help to rub it in by reminding them of the fact. Instead the lost need hope from a guide they can trust. If you are sinking in quicksand, you don't need to know the exact chemical composition of the substance or the precise workings of gravity and suction that are slowly dragging you down—what you long for is a rescuer who is standing on solid rock.

If our first understanding of God is more about his anger and judgement than about his love, mercy and generosity, it is not only natural but indeed inevitable that we come to outwork these values ourselves. If we believe that God doesn't 'take' to those outside the church, we too, in turn, will begin to despise or patronize them. Each of us is made in the image of our god; our view of God's character will reflect itself in our attitudes, behaviour, tone and body language. Behaviour is always the echo of belief.

Clearly at present something about the way many churches present the gospel simply turns people off. They don't see how our gospel equates with anything that might bear the label 'good news'. They have seen what the church has to offer and, frankly, are not interested. At one and the same time, the opportunity for the church has never been greater, and the relevance of the church to whole swathes of the population has seldom been less.

None of this is to argue that the gospel of Christ does not bear a natural offense. From the very beginnings of the church, the gospel was understood to be controversial, scandalous and subversive—we serve a Saviour who was crucified for the good news he dared to bring. Indeed, in the following chapters we will explore some of the reasons for that offence—the upside-down values by which Christ called his followers to live. All too often, however, the unchurched many who are longing for their world to be turned upside down are offended by the wrong thing: the poor manners, rudeness or judgementalism of zealous Christians.

Jesus' story of the prodigal son is the tale of a boy who has deeply wronged his father; when he has run out of money and realises that his life is screwed up, he turns and heads for home simply because he has nowhere else to go. When he arrives home he is not met with a sermon. He endures no recriminations, 'lessons we can learn from this' or 'I told you so's'. His father does not come out with a 'So you think you can walk back in here like nothing ever happened, do you? Well, it's just not that easy!' speech. Instead the son is met with open arms, love, celebration and forgiveness before it's been asked for; the fatted calf is killed in his honour, and a great party is thrown.

God gently woos those who do not yet know him—should our churches not do the same? God comes to embrace, not to bully. He is a lover, not a rapist. The gospel of the big stick is no gospel at all. It is time for our churches to more fully embrace a gospel whose first gentle note is love.

SOCIAL CREATURES

A great craving of our age is for meaning through community. In the film *The Shawshank Redemption* one of the characters (an old man named Brooks Hatlan) is released from the prison that has been his home for most of his life. He finds himself in a world he doesn't recognise; he longs for his old life back in prison, where, although he didn't have freedom, he had friends. In a letter 'home' to his buddies in Shawshank he says, 'The world went and got itself in a big damn hurry.'

In a particularly moving scene we find out that Brooks would rather kill himself than live as an alien in the modern world. Authorities, no doubt, locked Brooks up under the belief that he belonged in prison — it only took time, though, for prison to become the place where even he felt he belonged. In prison, another of the inmates observes, '[Brooks was] an important man, an educated man. A librarian. Out there, he's nothing.' The sudden dislocation from his friends, his identity and his home leaves him unable to cope. Ultimately he commits suicide.

Millions of people feel like Brooks Hatlan. We live in a high-speed world full of labour-saving technologies, and we never seem to have enough hours in the day. Though our impressive new communications mean that we can be in contact with anyone we choose in an instant, more and more of us live in isolation. A great many people feel that they have lost their sense of belonging. It is interesting to note that the statistics for suicide reveal that worldwide young men (ages fifteen to thirty-four) are the most vulnerable group — and in my experience they are also the least likely to be found in church.

Could the church find some means of offering these people the very thing they crave? The answer must be yes, but for some reason we aren't doing it.

The church is to be a reflection of God, and God is a trinity. As Paul Tillich commented, 'The doctrine of the Trinity is the fullest expression of man's relation to God.' The human capacity for relationships (albeit fractured and frail relationships), both with each other and with God, is a facet of our being made in the image of God. But more than this: if God is community, a person can never become his or her true self in isolation apart from society. Humanity is designed with not only the capacity but also the need for community. Genuine personhood is something that we can enter into only by means of relationship with others.

Loneliness did not prompt God to create the universe. God, because he is Trinity, cannot be lonely. He is three persons in perfect relationship and communication. Rather, it was the perfection of this tri-personal love and interdependence that inspired creation—the desire to share his relationship. For that reason, in the words of Leonardo Boff, 'human society is a pointer on the road to the mystery of the Trinity, while the mystery of the Trinity, as we know it from revelation, is a pointer toward [human] social life.'

Loneliness, as Mother Teresa once observed, is one of the most prevalent and depressing diseases of the Western world. We live in a culture that often feels acutely impersonal and alienating. Recently the body of a sixty-three-year-old man was found by police, having been undiscovered in his home for six years. An overwhelming number of people feel like no more than an account number to a bank, a policy reference to an insurance company, a tax code or a license number or a faceless statistic to the government. 'I am not a number, I am a free man' was the famous cry of Patrick McGoohan, star of the 1960s cult television series *The Prisoner*. The tragedy is that his words serve as the cry of countless millions of people, both young and old, in the villages, towns and cities across our planet today.

If we live in a world that is at least open to and quite possibly desperate for spiritual input and authentic community, why is the church declining in numbers? Something must have gone very wrong indeed. The fields are ripe for harvest, but it seems we've locked ourselves in the farmhouse.

RESCUERS

Often when Christians see figures of declining church attendance, we have a tendency to panic and rush around trying to save church from extinction. The truth is that we have spent so much time worrying about how we will save our churches, networks and denominations (our beloved institutions) that we often lose sight of our true task — to serve and save the world.

The simple truth is that the world doesn't owe us anything. Wider society is not responsible for the upkeep of our buildings, for filling our pews or for funding our charitable projects. The world was not, is not and never will be beholden to the church. The world does not exist for the church but the church for the world.

It's ironic but true that in serving the world more fully, the church, in whatever form it takes, will be rendered immune from extinction. A saved world would certainly result in a saved church. The reverse is not necessarily true. If we huddle in our trenches (however well equipped they may be) making occasional forays farther afield to win converts in order to bolster our numbers, we are condemned to watch as the church, and the world along with it, perishes.

We cannot attempt to maintain the status quo while simultaneously hoping for radical change. Jesus said, 'Whoever wants to save his life will lose it' (Matthew 16:25). Our desire to hang on to our institutions may well prove to be the very thing that wrests them from our grasp. If we wish to save our churches, surely we must lay them down.

The world doesn't owe us anything, but we do owe the world our service. The introverted question, 'Does God's church have a mission?' needs to be stood on its head: 'Does God's mission have a church?' Bringing hope to the world, and in so doing demonstrating his love for it and ours for him, must be our priority.

Søren Kierkegaard, the famous Danish Christian philosopher, grew up in the countryside surrounded by farms that reared geese (among other animals). Each spring he would watch as a new gaggle of goslings was hatched and began to be fattened for the table. Over the course of their short lives these geese would gorge themselves at constantly refilled troughs of grain until they were so fat they could hardly walk. He imagined that they believed their lives to be perfect, as every need they had was catered in abundance.

When autumn came, the truth became apparent. The wild geese that had spent the warm summer months in Denmark would gather in preparation for their southerly migration. As they assembled to fly south they would circle in the skies above the farms, calling out to any stragglers to join in their flight. At this point the farmed geese would lift their heads from the feeding troughs and look into the skies, heeding the call of their wild cousins. For the first time in their lives they would become animated, running as best they could around their enclosures and attempting to fly. Of course, their gluttonous diet and life of luxury meant that they were far too fat to get airborne — but still they would try. And then, as quickly as the commotion had started, the wild geese would fly off and the fattened farm geese would watch them briefly before returning to their grain to continue eating their way to their deaths.

Kierkegaard's parable poses a powerful challenge to our local churches. Are we farmed geese or wild geese?

Consider, for example, the healthcare industry: Whether a country provides free medical health service or requires citizens to purchase medical insurance, the purpose of medical professionals is to serve those in need. The problem is that the focus is sickness rather than health. The point at which any one of us engages with the health professionals is when we are ill. When do you make an appointment with the doctor? When do see a psychiatrist? When do you go to the hospital or see a specialist? Answer: When you are sick.

What we need is a complementary service to exist alongside medical professionals that will keep people healthy. That service must be holistic. The old idea of separating the physical from the spiritual must be seen for what it is—a failed method of approaching illness let alone health. It fails simply because it refuses to acknowledge the reality of the way in which people are wired—whole people. Our physical health, mental health and spiritual health are interconnected; struggle in one area inevitably leads to struggle in another. For instance, the links between depression and self-worth, hope, fulfilment and good relationships are strong. A correlation exists between the rate of recovery from a serious illness and that person's sense of purpose, value and belonging. Problems such as obesity are linked to self-esteem and self-discipline. The world needs a true health service—a movement that promotes holistic, physical, social and spiritual well-being. The church should be that movement.

ORIENTATION

I would venture to say that the usual suggestions for sorting out our troubles may be shortsighted—it's going to take more than high-energy sermons, trendy songs and plush seats to revive our churches. But the minor doctrinal differences that separate the denominations cannot be the source of our problems either. Though I am a member of a denomination that is currently experiencing some limited growth, I do not believe that this is due to a special superiority of Baptist doctrine or a particular weakness in, say, Methodist doctrine. (It has been suggested that, assuming the current haemorrhage is not arrested, the last candle in the Methodist Church in the United Kingdom will be snuffed out in 2037.)

The problem is bigger than that. The church today is not looking to where it wants to be and setting out purposefully to get there. We must change our orientation. Tom Peters says, 'Always start with the end in mind.'

We tend to think about the altar or stage (and all that happens around it) as the front of the church building. As a result, the employees of a local church have been considered the frontline practitioners of the faith for generations. If the church is a metaphorical circle facing inwards, then the pastor and staff team are bound to be perceived as being at the centre and the front—and it is natural that we should look to the minister as the main player on the spiritual front line.

If, however, the people in the congregation all turn around and regard the doors through which they will exit as the front, suddenly those closest the doors are the ones leading the charge. When the circle is recast facing outwards, the leaders, as important as their roles are, are now seen in true perspective—central, outward facing, but not frontline. Church leaders are like team coaches—equipping their players for action. The strategy comes from the bench or dugout, but the action is always on the field.

Theodore Roosevelt noted in a speech given at the Sorbonne in Paris in 1910:

> It is not the critic who counts, not the man who points out how the strong man stumbled, or where the doer of deeds could have done better. The credit belongs to the man who is actually in the arena, whose face is marred by dust and sweat and blood, who strives valiantly, who errs and comes short again and again, who knows the great enthusiasms, the great devotions, and spends himself in a worthy cause, who at best knows achievement and who at the worst if he fails at least fails while daring greatly so that his place shall never be with those cold and timid souls who know neither victory nor defeat.

All Christians should find themselves on the frontline — we are each players in bringing God's kingdom.

An effective church is an intelligent church.

YES, BUT HOW?

The real problem for Christian mission in the West is not the absence of spiritual hunger in our postmodern society but rather the inability to engage with this longing. Even when we do recognise this hunger, often we aren't willing or able to respond in terms other than those dictated by existing traditions and structures.

This challenge is not new. Christians today face the same kind of paradigm-shifting decisions that confronted the apostle Peter as he considered what non-Jewish, Gentile Christianity might look like in the first century. Through his encounter with Cornelius, the Roman centurion in Acts 10, Peter had to learn that faithfulness to Scripture does not necessarily mean doing things the same way they've always been done. Instead, biblical faithfulness calls for a humble recognition that the Holy Spirit may still have more to teach us than we have, so far, been able to receive. Ironically, it is only by way of this kind of thoroughgoing and courageous reimagining of what it means to be the church in our new environment that we will remain firmly rooted in the historic tradition of our faith. It's this intelligent and scripturally faithful reimagining of church for the beginning of the twenty-first century that the rest of this book explores as we ask again what it means to allow our Christology to determine our missiology and our missiology to shape our churches.

O   O   O

QUESTIONS

1. If your church runs small groups, ask leaders to discuss the following statement: Albert Einstein once commented that 'the kind of thinking that will solve the world's problems will be of a different order to the kind of thinking that created those problems in the first place.'

2. Do you see dissonance between your church's form and its function?

3. What are the nonnegotiables of church — what are the things that make a church a church?

4. What opportunities and challenges do you think the emergence of post-modern culture present to your local church?

CHAPTER 2

INCLUSIVE
CHURCH

A n intelligent church is an inclusive church. Inclusion is essentially the task of working with and involving others — counting them in rather than out.

The fact that the Bible exists at all says something extremely significant about God. That it is a big book, not a pamphlet, speaks volumes about God's nature and style. God has something to say to us, and he is determined to say it. From Genesis, where God walks and talks with Adam in the garden of Eden, to Revelation, where he reassures us of his presence and his plans, he never stops communicating with us — counting us in.

THE INCARNATION

The epicentre of the biblical story is the incarnation — the account of how God became human and walked on the earth. Jesus of Nazareth was fully man and, at one and the same time, fully God. That God came to a dirty cave in a dusty Middle-Eastern town as a fragile baby is an emphatic statement about his desire for engagement, relationship and involvement with his creation. God comes to where we are, speaks our language and wears our clothes — surely the greatest act of including the universe has ever seen. This central act of all history has huge

31

only if by incarnation we mean the whole
of christ event

implications for the way in which we understand and relate to God, for the way in which we think of ourselves and of others, and for the way in which we imagine society.

Through the incarnation, God accommodated himself to us. Not only did he speak to his creation—he became a part of it. Though humanity had consistently turned its backs on the Creator, he still came to draw his people back. Though he would have been justified in abandoning us, instead he came even closer in order that he might include us in his plans. Through Jesus, Michael Lloyd points out,

> God has become part of his world. He has entered into its dimensions, its physicality, its chronology, its life, its set of inter-relationships and constraints. He is here within it. He has always been present within it, of course, but not as part of it before. Something new and dramatic and eternal has happened which is relevant to every particle of matter and every moment of time. And this new, dramatic, eternal, cosmic event is accessible and comprehensible and relatable-to, because it is a human event, a birth, a life event for a peasant girl—and the Life Event for all that is. He has become one of us.

If absolutely nothing of the teachings of Jesus or the accounts of his miracles were recorded, we would still learn a great deal about how to be a church simply from this central fact: God became a man. He stood where we stand, shared our world, our emotions, our pain and our humanity. His model for communication is involvement. God's model for inclusion does not demand that we journey to him to meet him on his terms and his turf but rather reveals that he journeys to us to meet us on our turf and in our culture.

THE TEMPLE

One of the most striking stories about Jesus is that of the cleansing of the Temple in Jerusalem (Matthew 21; Mark 11; John 2). It is often assumed that the point of this story is the injustice of the excessive profit made in the house of God. However, on closer examination we see that it's a battle *for* inclusion, not simply *against* inflation.

In Jesus' day the Jewish establishment was far from inclusive. Theirs was a culture littered with outcasts. A repressive but effective social hierarchy was firmly in place. People were either acceptable or unacceptable, clean or unclean, in or out, included or excluded. The physically disabled, tax collectors, slaves, Gentiles, prostitutes and, to a degree, all women were considered beyond the pale. The unclean, it was believed, contaminated the cleanliness of others — so the pious had to be extremely careful not to come into contact with outcasts. And right at the heart of this system of exclusion stood the Temple, because the Temple and all it stood for were right at the heart of Israel.

For the Jews, the Temple was God's dwelling place on earth, quite literally 'the house of the Lord'. N. T. Wright explains it this way:

> The Temple was ... the heart and centre of Judaism, the vital symbol around which everything else circled. It was supposed to be the place where God himself dwelt, or at least had dwelt and would do so again. It was the place of sacrifice, not only the place where sins were forgiven but also the place where the union and fellowship between Israel and her god was endlessly and tirelessly consummated. It was, not least because of these two things, the centre of Israel's national and political life.

Small wonder then that Jesus' attack on the Temple was seen as something of a sensation!

The whole Temple site was considered sanctified ground, but it was regarded as increasingly holy or sacred the deeper one got into the building. On the periphery was the Court of the Gentiles, which was accessible to Gentiles and Jews alike. This was the temple's outer courtyard where the money changers did their business by exchanging Roman cash for temple currency—the only coinage that enabled the faithful to buy animals for sacrifice. Forgiveness did not come cheap in Jerusalem. The next area of the Temple was designated the Court of Women, accessible only to Jews, including their wives and children (though anyone with a visible disability was barred). Farther in again came the Court of the Jews, which was open only to Jewish men. Beyond this came a closely guarded section of the Temple, accessible only to the priests, containing the altar for the sacrifice of animals. At the centre of the Temple was the Holy of Holies, the inner sanctum, the place in which God was believed to be incarnate on earth. The Holy of Holies, which was shielded behind a curtain, could be accessed only by the high priest—and even he was restricted to one visit per year.

The effect of this hierarchy was that the people who most needed to encounter the God of love (the outcasts, the physically disabled, the poor, the Gentiles, the women and children) were unable to gain access to the only place in which they could meet him. God was more securely guarded than any president or king in history. In this way the Temple functioned as a gigantic filtration system—an exclusion machine that mirrored Jewish society under the boot of the priests and Pharisees.

The Temple-cleansing story—Jesus battling against the unfair and unjust regime of the day—is really all about God's rejection of, and anger at, this exclusion.

When Jesus turned over the money changers' tables, the Temple was thrown into chaos, and, temporarily at least, the system ground to a halt. Matthew records the resulting confusion: those who were blind and lame pushed right past the guards and rushed into the Temple to find Jesus; he healed them, and did so without the need for animal sacrifice on their part. Not only was this an act of inclusion; it was also an act of revolution. It was a demonstration of Christ's messianic values—throwing down the gauntlet to the old guard. Jesus had come to destroy their stranglehold and announce that the kingdom of God was available to all. It was a declaration of intent.

The Temple cleansing was not a sudden spur-of-the-moment idea or the action of a hotheaded rebel. Jesus was making a deliberate stand for the poor and excluded. And, as the account in John's gospel proves, it was carefully considered. 'So he made a whip out of cords, and drove all from the Temple area, both sheep and cattle; he scattered the coins of the money changers and overturned their tables' (John 2:15). The fact that Jesus plaited cords into a whip before confronting the money changers removes any lingering doubt that this was not a deliberate, premeditated act.

Acts 3 records that after Jesus' death and resurrection, Peter and John, two of Jesus' disciples and leaders of the church in Jerusalem, were walking to the Temple to pray. By the gate called Beautiful—the entrance from the courtyard into the Court of Women—they met a man who was unable to walk and reduced to begging for survival. Being disabled, he was also barred from further access to the Temple. Unable to offer him the money he was pleading for, the two gave him a much more precious gift—physical healing. The man's response was to run and jump and praise God—entering ground that had previously been firmly off-limits to him.

This healing was an act of inclusion: someone who had previously been relegated to the margins of Israel's spiritual life was brought into the fold. Equally significant is the fact that Peter and John healed the man outside the Temple walls—reinforcing the fact that the Temple was no longer the only arena of God's presence and activity.

Matthew's gospel goes on to record that at the time of Jesus' death on the cross, the curtain in the Temple that guarded the Holy of Holies was torn in two from top to bottom (Matthew 27:51). This signified that God was available to everyone everywhere. He was with his people—not confined to the prison of the religious building or institution. And, as if to highlight the point, just a few years later the Temple itself was completely destroyed. There was no longer a building of bricks and mortar—however grand—anywhere that was considered God's house.

SEGREGATION

The Jewish establishment had effectively developed a society of apartheid. But, though it is easy and obvious to draw comparisons between first-century Israel and twentieth-century South Africa, in reality Israel was by far the more segregated society. Prior to the early 1990s South Africans committed some heinous crimes (often in the name of Christianity) and segregated their society on one marker—that of race. Israel's segregation, on the other hand, was multilayered; discrimination existed on the basis of race, occupation, physical appearance, gender and age. Those who were not acceptable on any of these counts were marginalized socially and religiously. But it was into this world of apartheid and exclusion that Jesus was born—with a gospel that was good news.

Early on in his ministry, Jesus earned the disapproval of Israel's religious leaders for openly spending time with the very people whom they had intentionally and deliberately shunned. Not only did he welcome these outsiders; he touched them and even ate with them—he included them in.

But Jesus' attitude did far more than transform individual lives by showing them the acceptance they had so long been denied. It cut deeper. It began to challenge the legitimacy of the dominant social and religious structures. By his actions, Jesus was declaring war on the system. Those who had previously been excluded in the name of God, the spiritual outcasts, were now being drawn into relationship with him—much to the dismay of the pious priests and Pharisees.

The truth, of course, is that the people of God were always supposed to be inclusive—as a glance in a biblical concordance under the headings 'Refugee', 'Widows' or 'Fatherless'

quickly reveals. But more than that, right from the start, with
the account of the creation, the covenant with Noah (Genesis
6), the choosing of Abraham for the benefit of all peoples on
earth (Genesis 12), the covenant with David (1 Samuel 16)
and onward, we encounter through the Bible a God who not
only claims to be Lord of all but who has laid out a plan for
all of his world and its peoples. The Old Testament relentlessly
announces Yahweh's universality.

Tragically, the people Israel made the mistake of trying to
guard the purity of their faith by distancing themselves from
people of all other religions. They also fell into the trap of misunderstanding the privilege they enjoyed as the people of God.
They considered their relationship with God to be exclusive
and accepted little or no responsibility toward the rest of the
peoples of the world. The stubbornness of Jonah and his reluc-
tance to preach to the people of Nineveh is just one graphic
symbol of this tragic attitude.

The people of Israel tried to domesticate God. They turned
Yahweh into their own local and tribal god—the god of the
Jews—and if you weren't Jewish you couldn't get to know him
except by becoming one of them.

WORLDLY INFLUENCE

The attitude of exclusivity is a mistake that has often been
repeated by the church—that of setting ourselves apart in the
name of preserving the truth. We don't want to be contaminated by the corrupting influences of our world.

A friend of mine is the vicar of a high Anglican Church.
One Saturday morning a member of his congregation, a church
warden, came to his door in a state of desperate panic. He
invited her in to find out what was wrong and what he could
do to help. As soon as they were inside she began her story:
That morning she had collected a box of communion wafers
for the next day's Eucharist service. She had put the wafers

carefully into her handbag and caught the bus home. But when she arrived back at her house she discovered that the box had somehow opened in her bag; the wafers had spilled out and broken into countless pieces. Not knowing what to do she went straight to the vicar's house, still clutching the bag filled with the crumbs of Christ's body.

Having heard her story, my friend sympathized that it was a shame the wafers had been broken, but said that it really wasn't something to get in a panic about as they could always get some more. 'But you don't understand,' said the woman, still notice-ably agitated. Staring into the handbag at the crushed wafers, she pondered, 'It's just that ... Has my handbag contaminated the host, or has the host sanctified my handbag?'

The story may be lighthearted, but it illustrates a serious question for the church—do we believe that involvement in secular society corrupts and contaminates us? Who can we safely include in our communities? Where do we draw the line? Should we draw a line? If we don't, will we be com-promised and lose our distinctives? After all, standards matter! Should we withdraw and safeguard ourselves and the truth we hold?

The greatest compromise is that of withdrawal, and the greatest loss of Christian distinctiveness is that which comes from a lack of involvement. In truth, withdrawal is invariably a sign not of confidence but of insecurity and a lack of inner strength. Authentic, intelligent church is inclusive church, and it always has been. The task of the followers of Christ is to include all those marginalized by the religious and political machine, to create community by welcoming in those who have faith outside the boundaries of traditional religious respectability, to offer hope to all those who long for God. Yes, standards matter. And this is the standard we are called to uphold at all cost—the standard that proclaims the starting place is that of God's grace and inclusion.

INCARNATIONAL

If God is incarnational, and the church's task is to be part of God's mission, this principle must become ours too. An inclusive church will be a congregation open to all — a community for those displaced. It will be an environment in which the unloved and the unlovely find refuge and belonging. It will be a refuge to the homeless, a family to the forgotten, a friend to the lonely and a place where the outcasts of society can enjoy life in all its fullness.

An inclusive church will not be made up only of people who have life sorted. Instead it will almost certainly include drug users, alcoholics, people with mental health problems, the homeless, the unemployed, single mothers, ex-convicts, prostitutes and so on. It will be a church where the imperfect are perfectly welcome. It will strive to ensure that it is accessible to those who can't walk, or hear, or see or speak. In short, it will be a home for those who need one.

It is a mistake and a misreading of the New Testament to equate the church's mission simply with the poor in the sense of economic deprivation. It is striking that even in Luke's gospel, with its heightened emphasis on Christ's mission to the socially and economically excluded, he is repeatedly found in the homes of the wealthy (for example, 5:29; 7:36; 14:1; 19:5). Who are the poor, and what constitutes poverty? In the New Testament poverty is not simply defined by economics. The story of Jesus and Zacchaeus represents a clear example of this. Financially Zacchaeus was more than comfortable — but spiritually his poverty and exclusion were deep. The church's definition of poverty and exclusion is far broader than any government's; our mission, therefore, is more inclusive than that of any statutory social welfare department.

God, in Jesus, adopts a form we can recognise and identify with. He accepts the limitations of humanity in order that he might communicate with us in terms that we can understand. He accommodates himself to us. Indeed, any human language about or discussion of God is accommodating. It is impossible to sum up the Creator of all things using human concepts and language. God comes to people, meeting them where they are rather than expecting them to come to him. Indeed even one of Jesus' names, Emmanuel, means 'God with us'.

The story of the day of Pentecost is another wonderful illustration of how God accommodates himself to us — of how his inclusion of us begins with his journeying to meet us on our turf. When the Holy Spirit fell on Jesus' followers they all 'began to speak in other tongues as the Spirit enabled them' (Acts 2:4). But why the gift of speaking in tongues? Over the centuries the gift of tongues has proved to be utterly contentious within local church life. So why does God grant this — not some other less controversial sign of his presence?

To answer this question we must first look at Jesus' words to his disciples in Matthew 28. Here he sets out for his followers his radical agenda — what we now refer to as the Great Commission. Their task was to go to all nations and make disciples. But the word *ethnos*, which we have translated as 'nation', is more accurately translated 'ethnic-group' or even 'tribe'. In other words it defines people by their language, customs, beliefs, morals, values and culture rather than by their geography or country of residence. Jesus is calling his followers to take the issue of ethnicity and situation seriously and to work with it and respect it rather than be blind to it or attempt to ignore it.

It is this principle that is underlined in Acts 2 when, on receiving the Holy Spirit, the same disciples are given the ability to speak in tongues. These are not, however, the heavenly languages that the church has so often argued about over the centuries. How do we know? Because verse 5 makes it absolutely clear. It explains that Jews from every nation under heaven were staying in Jerusalem and listening to Peter and his friends, and that when they began to speak in other tongues the response was, 'Are not all these men who are speaking Galileans? Then how is it that each of us hears them in his own native language?' (Act 2:7–8). God's vision clearly takes diversity seriously and affirms, not obliterates, the obvious differences of those present.

But here is the twist. All those who had gathered in Jerusalem on that day could speak the same language. How do we know that? Because they were all Jews. Hebrew was the common language of the Jews, and Greek was the official language of the Eastern Roman Empire. So two perfectly good global languages that the disciples were fluent in could have been used to communicate to the crowds that day. But God met the people using the words that they learnt on their mother's knee — the words and phrases that they thought and dreamt in.

Perhaps the greatest miracle of Pentecost is this: God chooses to speak to us in our own language. His is no one-size-fits-all policy. He comes to us. He begins where we are.

If the incarnation is God personally involving himself with his people, the day of Pentecost is God miraculously equipping the church to do the same. The rest of the book of Acts is the story of how the first Christians connected with the world, slowly discovering how to contextualize the gospel for each people group they encountered — to meet them on their own turf.

This same task remains the challenge for the church today: to start where people are, to engage in our communities, to embrace the public — in short, to speak their language.

ATTRACTIONAL

In the twentieth century much of the church fell into the trap of relying on an attractional model: 'Come to us. You know where we are.' In recent years, however, the focus has begun to shift to an incarnational model. Much has been written on the subject of incarnational mission, and many of its proponents advocate churches moving out of their dusty steepled buildings and into their communities.

It's a vital and compelling message, but we do well to remember that truth flies on two wings. The promotion of incarnational mission should not be synonymous with the denigration of the attractional model. We need both.

Jesus was a phenomenally attractive man. Yes, God came to earth. Yes, Jesus went to the outcasts. But people were also drawn to him. Characters like Zacchaeus would not be featured in the Gospels had Jesus not stirred their curiosity. Something about Jesus caused people to want to be around him. They liked him. He was good company, so much that they came from miles to be with him. His presence was magnetic.

Take the Sermon on the Mount. It would be difficult to imagine anyone trekking up a mountainside to hear a boring sermon delivered by an uncharismatic man—especially in the context of first-century Judea where another sermon from another spiritual leader would be just a moment away. Or think about his first miracle, that of turning water into wine, which took place at a wedding in Cana—Jesus was the kind of man people wanted to invite to parties even before they knew about his unusual gift for wine making. Children loved him; people trusted him.

How do people feel about the church today?

In order to reflect God's inclusiveness, our mission is to be both incarnational and attractive. An inclusive church will be the kind of community to which people will want to belong. Our task is to meet people where they are but also to provide the attraction of facilities and services that draw them to us. (Our buildings can be some of our greatest assets.) Our mission is both come and go, never either/or, always both/and.

At Church.co.uk, Waterloo, the church of which I am the senior minister, we have tried many different ways of getting

involved with our local community. One of the most successful is our coffee shop, 'Taste'. It was a simple idea: we adapted
the front of the church (even converting the old pulpit into a
bar), bought the necessary equipment, and began selling fairly
traded coffee—lattes, cappuccinos, mochas and Americanos—at
reasonable prices to passersby. To begin with, Taste was entirely
staffed by volunteers from our church congregation; but over
time, as relationships have grown, many of our staff are people
who originally came in for one cup of coffee and have stayed.
Taste has become a little community (or congregation) in its
own right, with many regulars coming in to drink our coffee,
use the Internet, build friendships and offer and receive support
to and from one another. We've begun to see individual lives
changed as people have developed relationships with each other
and with Christ. Taste's strength is that it is incarnational—we're
meeting people where they are and talking to them in their
own language—but it is also attractional, as literally hundreds
of people who would normally never set foot over the doorstep
come into our building and, over time, have often moved on to
one of our worship services.

Above all we need to be available. Our church buildings should
still be places of sanctuary. The truth is, of course, that most people's
personal crises do not take place while the local church service is
in full swing on a Sunday morning (and even if they did, and they
had the confidence to turn up and tell us, it would usually be seen
as an interruption). If our churches are truly to be inclusive, we
need to be available twenty-four hours a day, seven days a week.
We each need to undertake the task of reestablishing our churches
as the hub of the community. And it is our responsibility to ensure
that nobody, save by his or her own choice, is left out. That means
that those of us who have buildings need to think hard about the
what, when, how and why of their use. What messages do our
buildings deliver just as the Temple did in Israel? In what ways do
they symbolize our attitude to our society?

Inclusion begins when we realise that all we are, have and do belongs to God. As American poet Maya Angelou has observed, 'Life is God's gift to us; what we do with it is our gift to him.' Each of the 168 hours in a week belongs to God—an inclusive church understands this principle. We must love unconditionally and give our time selflessly. To be Jesus to people is simply to love them as they are and to help them achieve fullness of life here and now. It is to be open and honest about who we are—to share the whole of our lives.

An intelligent church is an inclusive church.

YES, BUT HOW?

How can we go about meeting people where they are? How do we speak to others in their native languages? In what ways can our church's mission begin to imitate God's inclusive ways of working?

In their book *The Shaping of Things to Come*, Michael Frost and Alan Hirsch tell the story of a man who has found a way to speak to the people of San Francisco in their own language:

> The Subterranean Shoe Room is a very cool retro-shoe store in the hippest part of perpetually cool San Francisco. It was opened on Valencia Street this year by an unlikely proprietor. Brock Bingaman is a Southern Baptist church planter/ evangelist who came to San Francisco with every intention of planting a conventional purpose-driven type church. He had planted churches before and one conversation with him reveals that he is an evangelist to the core. But San Francisco is crawling with failed conventional purpose-driven type church planters. So secular, so culturally vigorous, so pro-gay is the city that the conventional churches are withering on the vine. Crestfallen, young Brock realised that there was no point trying to re-create what many had tried and failed at before him. Needing gainful employment, Brock says he turned to his first love—shoes!

You see, Brock is the Imelda Marcos of the Southern Baptist Convention. Ever since he was a boy, he has collected shoes. He loves the darn things. When we told him we only own two or three pairs each, he scoffed. 'I buy two or three pairs a week!' he laughed. Together with his brother Josh and their wives, he rented a shop and filled it with new and retro (restored second-hand) shoes. Now he's doing a roaring trade in a fashion district that until the Subterranean Shoe Room opened only had a sports shoe outlet.

Brock has a special gift when it comes to shoes, though. He's no ordinary shoe salesman. He strikes up a conversation with those who browse his collection, and when they tell him they're not sure what they're looking for, he has a standard retort: 'Tell me about yourself and I'll tell you the shoes you need.' And so scores of San Franciscans have opened their lives to him. After hearing their story, Brock tells them he has just the thing they're looking for and pulls out a pair of pink Pumas or cherry-red Docs. And he seems to get it right every time.

'As a church planter, I spent ninety per cent of my time with Christians,' he moans. 'Now, as a shoe salesman, I spend ninety per cent of my time with non-Christians.' He has developed significant relationships with gay couples, Marxist professors, aging hippies and bohemian artists. Just the kind of people you don't find in church.... It's a tough town to evangelize, and Brock has struck on a natural way to incarnate the message of the gospel to a people group normally hostile to Christianity.

○   ○   ○

QUESTIONS

1. If your church runs small groups, ask leaders to spend some time with their groups over the next month asking the question, 'How can we become more inclusive?' Once all the groups have reported back, list the five most common themes. Talk together as a church leadership

about practical ways in which you can address the issues. Put it all together in a special newsletter and distribute it to the congregation or make it the subject of a month's preaching and teaching.

2. If you have not already done so, carry out an access audit for your church building. This will tell you how to make your building inclusive of people with disabilities. Go beyond that and contact local disability groups to ask them to help you with your audit. Once you have a plan of action, let people know that your building is accessible by using the international symbols for disability on your literature, your signs and your Web site.

3. Carry out a community audit and a church audit. The first will help you to understand what the real needs of your community are and will also let you know what is already going on in your community. The second will help you to identify the strengths and weaknesses of your congregation. Once you have this information, you can work out the best way forward.

4. Adopt the Faithworks charter (see page 181). It establishes goals and objectives for being an inclusive church and helps you to understand the practical issues you will face as you embark on this journey.

5. Take a look at your church leadership. Does it reflect the community? Does it reflect the people in your congregation? When you select or appoint new leaders, choose leaders who will broaden the experience of the team. Devise ways of making sure the leadership team listens to the congregation more.

CHAPTER 3

MESSY
CHURCH

An intelligent church is a messy church. Why? Because messiness is the consequence of being inclusive. Whenever a local church chooses to be outward-looking and welcoming of all, it will automatically become messier than it was before — it's inevitable.

Over the years I've heard an endless number of Christians enthuse longingly about getting back to a New Testament model of church. Those people may not realise that the early church struggled over issues of inclusion too; as a result, church life got messy for them as well. It's clear from Paul's letters to the Christians in Corinth, Galatia and Colossae that establishing, growing and sustaining a church was a demanding and messy business. In fact, all of the churches with whom Paul corresponded were struggling with different aspects of their faith and different issues within their congregations.

MESSY LEADERS

When I read the Gospels I never cease to be surprised and, at the same time, relieved by the limited understanding of the disciples — they constantly seem to miss the point of what Jesus is saying and doing. They have an inexhaustible capacity to get hold of the wrong end of the stick. They also have a habit of letting Jesus down—falling asleep in the garden of Gethsemane, for example. Even Peter, the rock upon which the church would be built, denied knowing Jesus to protect himself—in spite of the fact that he was outraged when Jesus suggested he would do exactly that.

The disciples, it is fair to say, were far from perfect. Yet it is to this rough band of working men that Jesus chose to entrust his continuing mission. Let us be in no doubt: God is happy to work with sinners.

A brief look at the group of twelve who followed Jesus most closely, recorded in Matthew 10, reveals a diverse bunch of men. Yet Jesus managed not only to hold them all together but to build them into a team. From Levi, the puppet of the Romans, to Simon the Zealot, who hated all that Rome stood for—each held different, even opposing, views; and each would have struggled with others within the group. But Jesus accepted them all and held them all together. Messy? Of course it was. Dynamic? Like nothing you've ever seen.

In Jesus' teaching, judgement is put on hold. He chooses to work with people as he finds them and allows the weeds to grow up with the wheat (Matthew 13). For example, none of the Gospels make any suggestion that Judas was distrusted or held at arm's length. He was loved and included just as much as the other disciples. That he would ultimately betray Jesus for a handful of coins does not seem to have limited his relationship with Jesus before the event. Judas opted out of relationship with God—but it was he who had to make that decision. Jesus did not turn him away or prematurely close the relationship. Even near the end, it seems that Jesus deliberately left the door open for Judas as long as possible; the one who was to be betrayed washed the betrayer's feet and shared a meal with him.

Very often we are guilty of making snap judgements that later prove to be wrong judgements. When ruffled we tend to react

instantly rather than responding thoughtfully and graciously.
Jesus, however, was willing to put up with mess and ambiguity
in order to make leaders out of losers. He gave people room to
grow and knew that some were late developers. He not only
saw the best in people but also gave them his best; and slowly,
in return, he often drew the best from them. The process must
have been painful, but the results were amazing.

When I started out as a minister at Tonbridge Baptist Church
I gained some understanding of working with messy people—I
ran a church youth group! The interesting thing about spending
time with the same group of kids month after month, year on year,
is that you tend to imagine what each of them will go on to do.
For instance, I was certain that a few of the young people in my
group would end up as church leaders in some shape or form—I
could see that they were people of unshakable, unswerving faith.
I was also privately convinced that one or two others would
get nowhere—they would fall by the wayside and possibly drag
others down with them. Over the years I discovered that I was
completely wrong. Many of the kids for whom I had such high
hopes have drifted far away from the church altogether, while
several of those I had written off not only became Christians
but are now serving Christ and inspiring me and many others
to get to know him better. You never can tell. I've seen enough
hopeless addicts find Christ and go on to great things and enough
respected church leaders throw away their lives, marriages and
ministries over sex, money or power to know that you can't tell
who will surprise you. The weeds and the wheat have to go
together—even though it's a messy way to grow a crop.

The apostle Paul wrote these words to his young friend
Timothy, the leader of the church in the city of Ephesus, with
some advice about how he should go about selecting leaders:

> Here is a trustworthy saying: If anyone sets his heart on
> being an overseer, he desires a noble task. Now the overseer

must be above reproach, the husband of but one wife, temperate, self-controlled, respectable, hospitable, able to teach, not given to drunkenness, not violent but gentle, not quarrelsome, not a lover of money. He must manage his own family well and see that his children obey him with proper respect. (If anyone does not know how to manage his own family, how can he take care of God's church?) He must not be a recent convert, or he may become conceited and fall under the same judgement as the devil. He must also have a good reputation with outsiders, so that he will not fall into disgrace and into the devil's trap.

Deacons, likewise, are to be men worthy of respect, sincere, not indulging in much wine, and not pursuing dishonest gain. They must keep hold of the deep truths of the faith with a clear conscience. They must first be tested; and then if there is nothing against them, let them serve as deacons.

In the same way, their wives are to be women worthy of respect, not malicious talkers but temperate and trustworthy in everything.

A deacon must be the husband of but one wife and must manage his children and his household well. Those who have served well gain an excellent standing and great assurance in their faith in Christ Jesus.

(1 Timothy 3:1–13)

On the surface this seems like fairly straightforward stuff. When you're choosing leaders steer clear of polygamists, drunks, crooks, street fighters and the like. And it is straightforward—until you consider that all of the above-mentioned people must have been part of the church that Timothy was leading. Paul's letter is practical and pastoral, not philosophical. It's highly unlikely that he would bother highlighting these issues if Timothy didn't know any such people.

Make no mistake: Timothy's was a messy church, just as any church that has mission at its heart will be. Life is messy, and therefore church life in our post-Christian society will be messy too. For this reason an inclusive church might not always be the most comfortable place for established Christians to be — but then who ever said that the church should be about making Christians comfortable?

MESSY PEOPLE

Our churches will never be messy until the messy people feel welcome — feel like they belong.

One of my friends leads a church in Wales. Noticing real problems of teenage pregnancy, drug abuse and prostitution in their town, they decided to set up a project to offer support and life-skills training to the young girls caught in this cycle. Over time a group of these young mums became interested in the wider life of the church and the message of Christianity — some of them just could not understand why people were so ready to serve and support them without any payment or reward.

The week before Mothering Sunday, one of the project workers invited them to the special Sunday morning Mother's Day service. Almost all of the girls expressed an interest in coming along but seemed slightly nervous. Eventually one of them plucked up the courage to raise the question that the others in the group had been silently thinking but didn't have the confidence to verbalize: 'Does your church have a side door?' The project worker was surprised. After hesitating she explained that it did but wondered about the relevance of the building's architecture. 'Well,' the girl explained, 'people like us aren't really the sort you want marching through the front door — proud as anything. We'll come, but we'd feel a lot better if we can come in through the side door so that nobody will notice us.'

We need to make lots of side doors for people, but we must also address the culture and message of our churches so that everyone will feel comfortable coming in our main entrances.

In many senses the church is a hospital—it is a place of spiritual, social, emotional, moral and psychological healing. And just as in a hospital the patients suffer from different conditions, are at different levels of health and are at different stages of the healing process, so it is with the church. Sometimes healing takes weeks or months—sometimes it takes a lifetime. Simply visiting a hospital doesn't automatically make a sick person well. Some need intensive care, others less intensive but no less important ongoing treatment or rehabilitation. No hospital is a centre of physical perfection, and neither is a church one of spiritual perfection—rather, both are messy environments full of messed-up people striving to be less so.

An ability to deal with messiness is a sign of spiritual maturity. Jesus' teachings, actions and attitudes all demonstrate his ease with and acceptance of the people around him. He was relaxed in the company of the disparate and disreputable bunch of people that followed him around. He was not fazed by being, or being seen, in the company of prostitutes, beggars, people with physical disabilities, despised ethnic groups or tax collectors—all of whom were considered sinners within Jewish society. More than that, he obviously liked these people, and because of him they dared to believe that they could be players in bringing the kingdom of God.

THE MESSAGE OF THE CHURCH

Why is it that so many people feel they don't belong in our churches? This is an important question and if we are serious about answering it and attempting to solve the problem it addresses, we must have the courage to look more honestly at the messages we send. We want to introduce the world to the God of love who is the solution to each individual's and every community's sin, isolation and dysfunction. The trouble is, rather than sending a message of hope around these issues, we've often ended up preaching, or being heard to preach, a debilitating and condemnatory message of judgement. As Homer Simpson once observed, 'I'm not a bad guy. I work hard and I love my kids. So why should I spend half my Sunday hearing about how I'm going to hell?'

Certain churches never fail to communicate that God has a big beef with humankind—that we can't seem to do anything right. They preach that from birth to death we are lost to sin and depravity and can do nothing of our own initiative to repair the broken relationship with God that results from our condition. Traditionally this has been known as the doctrine of original sin. As Augustine put it, according to Scripture, 'the deliberate sin of the first man is the cause of original sin'. Adam's sin in the garden of Eden caused a hereditary stain passed down to all humankind, with the result that every baby born is just as fallen, just as sinful by nature, as Adam and Eve after they were ejected from the garden.

I don't deny that the doctrine of original sin is biblically accurate but I do believe that getting our emphasis right is critically important. Because this message is often carelessly handled, countless people have received the impression that God doesn't really like humanity very much and that he is utterly disillusioned with us. I've given up trying to keep track of the number of people I have spoken to, young and old, who tell me, often through tears, 'I'm too sinful for God to ever be interested in me.' The double tragedy is that many of these are Christians who have been in our churches for years. Millions of people, both inside and outside the church, are paralyzed by the thought that God is angry with them and might smite them at any moment. Somehow we've been getting the wrong message across. And it's no good complaining that the people are simply hearing us wrong. Communication is never about what the sender thinks he or she is saying—it's all about what the receiver actually hears. The problem is ours, not theirs.

The doctrine of original sin takes the broken nature of our relationship with God seriously. However, when misapplied it denies or distorts a great and even more fundamental truth — original goodness. The God of love created us for relationship, loves us in a way that we can never begin to comprehend and declares that we bear his image (Genesis 1:26 – 31). Indeed, the first thing that God says about humanity is that it is 'very good'. If we are to embrace the doctrine of original sin, we must hold it in tension with the doctrine of original goodness. Only then will we understand — let alone preach — the greatest insight that the Bible offers about our Creator: God is love (1 John 4:8).

'Love is not a quality that God possesses, but the essence of God himself,' states Derek Tidball, principal of the London School of Theology, in his book *The Message of the Cross*. 'It is not a minor attribute that characterizes God on occasions, but the very heart of God, his essential being. It is not a component part of God, but his very nature. Before God is anything else, he is love.' God isn't disillusioned with humanity — he never had any illusions in the first place. Instead he loves us as we are and longs for us to work with him in re-creating the world. Nobody is too bad for God.

The misapplication of the doctrine of original sin leads to debilitated people with a deep sense of powerlessness and worthlessness. On a wider scale, it leads to a sense of fatalism that can destroy not just individuals but whole communities. 'If we are bound to get it wrong, then why try to change things at all? If our lives are fated from the outset, then how can that be our fault anyway?' This defeatism can be adequately dealt with only by communicating that, although we are affected by sin and have a propensity for wrong choices and actions, we are still 'fearfully and wonderfully made' (Psalm 139:14). We still bear the mark of our maker. God has invested something of his own glorious, beautiful nature in us.

If I am made in the image of God, then however much that image has been distorted, the image itself is still visible and recognisable. It is not destroyed by my sin. Early Christian writers universally believed that the *imago Dei* (image of God) remained present not just after the Fall of humanity but also whether or not a person chose to acknowledge God. Whatever the *imago Dei* consisted of, it was what constituted a person as a human being and therefore could not be lost. Augustine taught, 'Although worn out and defaced by losing the participation of God, yet the image of God still remains.' Each and every person, however far she has wandered from God, continues to bear the imprint of God in her life.

John Calvin used to talk of this image as being like a mirror that has been broken. A broken mirror will give you a messy image. But as we grow in our relationship with Christ, that brokenness is repaired and the image becomes clearer. The mirror may still be cracked, but it reflects an increasingly true image.

THE MISSION OF THE CHURCH

Understandably, many church people are often afraid of messiness in their safe haven, but when you consider the mission of the church, you realise that chaos isn't the problem. The problem is that some of our churches aren't very messy at all. I remember hearing an old businessman once comment, 'If it's neat, tidy, quiet and orderly that you're looking for, the graveyard is your only option.' Any church that truly welcomes anyone and everyone — whatever their problems and issues — is bound to appear (and indeed be) both chaotic and disorderly at times. What's wrong with being neat and tidy? The only problem is that it indicates that the church has scared the messed-up people away.

The very act of inclusion necessarily dictates that an intelligent church will be comprised of a disparate bunch of people who are at different points on the journey of faith. They will not believe the same things, have the same values or behave consistently. It would be much easier to run a community where the rules demanded that all of the members believed the same things, held the same values and behaved consistently. It would be easier, but it would be very small—and more important, it wouldn't be church. If we take Jesus as the model and invest ourselves in the lives of others as he did, our churches will never be neat, tidy or orderly.

Our mission is simply to reach out to others and walk with them as far as they will let us, taking them on a journey with God. And if we take this mission seriously, our churches will never look the same again. It's simultaneously a daunting, exciting, frustrating and fulfilling experience.

In all this there is another deeper truth. Jesus' command to us is clear: we are to love God and love our neighbour (Luke 10:27). Yes, we are told to 'go and make disciples of all nations' (Matthew 28:19), but the question remains: 'How do you make a disciple?' Christ's answer was simply 'teaching them to obey everything I have commanded you' (Matthew 28:20). In other words, Jesus told us to show everyone on earth that they should love God and love their neighbour—they should have a spirituality based upon an intimacy with God and an involvement in the lives of others.

That's it. That's all. It is not our job to convert people. Our job is to be intentional about showing God's love, grace and acceptance to people. Our task is to demonstrate his truth to those around us. Our duty is to love, serve and speak in Jesus' name. The rest is up to God. Too often we try to be the ones who do the convicting of people about their sin, highlighting their failings and trying to manoeuvre and manhandle them in the right direction. We need to be clear about one thing: we are not the Holy Spirit. Let's do our job and leave his to him. If we are truly to love our neighbours we must tolerate their inconsistencies and failings just as easily as we tolerate our own.

Over the years I have learnt that the most tolerant people are the most tolerable people. Tolerance is a truly attractive quality. Also, as Jesus points out, it is hard to take a good look at the speck of dust in your friend's eye when you have a plank in your own (Luke 6:41).

LIFE IN A MESSY CHURCH

A couple of years back I became the senior minister of Church.co.uk, Waterloo, in central London. When I arrived, the church (which was then called Christ Church and Upton Chapel) was struggling to survive. The morning service (which was the only real expression of church throughout the week) was attended by between ten and twenty-five people, including children. I can say without any hubris, as I am surrounded by a team of incredibly hardworking people, that in two years our church has been turned on its head. We are increasingly becoming the hub of our local community, and, although it is by no means the primary indicator of a church's worth, our morning (and now evening) congregation has multiplied by a factor of ten. Through the week small groups gather, youth clubs meet, the coffee shop is open to the public and any number of other projects are at various stages of development. But this growth, which has been largely due to our increased presence within the local community, has not been without difficulty.

Awhile ago I was confronted by one church member who wanted to complain about the fact that newcomers would stand on the church steps smoking before and after services. He was concerned that it was sending the wrong message. What he was really saying was that he was uncomfortable about the fact that things had become messier than they were in the good old days.

Just last week several drunk people (and their dog!) came into our morning service and caused absolute havoc—they shouted at the preacher, spilled their drinks on the carpet, and

sang a verse of a very different song than those we normally
sing on Sunday mornings. A few of our church members were
really upset.

One of those drunks was Bob. Bob has been regularly
coming to our coffee shop and spending lots of time chatting
with various members of staff. When he's not drunk he's a
lovely guy. But he's an alcoholic. He knows he has a problem
and is seeking professional care, which we are helping to sort
out for him. The reason he had brought his friends to our
morning service was that during the week he had told one of
our staff that his favourite song is 'Amazing Grace'. For him
it's not just a song. Bob has experienced amazing grace—he
really does consider himself a wretch and consequently feels
his salvation keenly. We promised him that on Sunday we'd
sing the song in church and he could stand with all of us and
join in with those words that mean so much to him. Sadly,
having stayed off the bottle all week, he had a drinking bout
on Saturday night.

Many people might have been uncomfortable about having
Bob and his friends staggering about the church building caus-
ing mayhem with their dog, embarrassment with their shouting
and offence with their bottles of cider. But we should feel more
uncomfortable if people like that don't feel they can come into
our churches.

So what did we do? One of our coffee shop staff helped
Bob and his mates through to another hall. We stopped what
we were doing in the service as I explained briefly who Bob is,
why he was with us and that we were trying to find him professional help to break free of his addiction. Finally we prayed
for him. As a result, after the service another member of the
congregation came to tell me about his secret addiction. And
the journey of salvation and freedom begins again.

When a couple marries and moves into their first home
together, they slowly establish a new order. They might dec-

orate the place and, over time, get new furniture. They will schedule time together and develop routines around daily life. However, as soon as a baby arrives that order is all but destroyed. Routines are disrupted and romantic evenings can no longer be guaranteed. The house is cluttered with all the paraphernalia that accompanies a newborn child. The new sofa will never look quite the same after it has been covered in vomit. And the time spent decorating to perfection seems wasted as walls, carpets and every stick of furniture are stained by one excretion or another. The old order and tidiness are lost from the house. But here is the miracle, as anyone who has gone through this process of change will attest: it has never been more of a home.

Any community that adds to its number will be changed by that addition. An inclusive church will be a messy church, and there will be those who find the transition uncomfortable. We cannot welcome people to our churches and then demand that they conform to our way of doing things—either instantly or even ultimately.

The aim of any church is never to be messy; it is to be inclusive. But who knows, learning to live with the messiness itself might just help us in our journey toward Christlikeness.

An intelligent church is a messy church.

YES, BUT HOW?

When churches are out of touch with the people who live around them, the problem is not that they are irrelevant—although they are—it is that they are not incarnational. Often the claim that 'we are a traditional church' is nothing more than a way of sidestepping the frank admission that 'we are not an incarnational church.' Our churches should be Christ-centred and follow his incarnational model of mission. Thus, to fail to address the needs of our surrounding community is not simply a cultural issue but a theological and, therefore, at its deepest level a spiritual issue—that of failing to address our biblical responsibility. We must embrace our neighbours and move forward with them as we seek to follow Christ. The great Catholic missionary and theologian Vincent Donovan wrote, 'Do not try to call them back to where they were, and do not try to call them to where you are, as beautiful as that place may seem to you. You must have the courage to go with them to a place neither you nor they have been before.'

O   O   O

QUESTIONS

1. As a leadership team, start to think about the things that are central to your identity—this is your ethos. Be completely honest in this exercise. It may be helpful to take your team away from the church for the day to address this issue. What preferences have you turned into dogmas? Be as hard on yourselves as you can. Talk about the ways in which you have allowed your guidelines to become tramlines and how you can meet this challenge.

2. Examine the partnerships you already have. Why did you choose to work with these groups? What can you learn from them? Are there other groups you could work with? Figure out how to go about becoming a church that works with others who are different.

3. Examine ways in which people can belong in the congregation even before they believe. You may need to think about the song choices, the format of the service and the way you greet people. Ask yourself what an outsider would feel like with the things you are preparing, and make adjustments as necessary.

4. If you preach or teach in the church, think about ways of connecting to those who do not normally come. Instead of trying to give people all the answers, explore ways of communicating that allow them to think things through for themselves. When preparing, try to represent a couple of views rather than just the one that you feel most comfortable with.

5. Get to know people who are not part of your church tradition. This might include people from the community or people from other traditions. As you get to know them, look for the things you can learn from them. As you do this, work out ways in which you could help and support them.

CHAPTER 4

HONEST
CHURCH

An intelligent church is an honest church. Honesty is a matter of integrity and authenticity. It is about making sure that what we say matches what we think and is reflected in what we do. Churches should be the most honest communities around.

I remember as a boy getting ready for the church service every Sunday morning. My mother would make me dress up for the occasion. I had to wear a suit, which would have been fine had it not been made out of the most hideous tartan fabric. If I felt ridiculous walking to church, I'm sure it was nothing compared to how ridiculous I looked.

One Sunday I plucked up the courage to ask my mum why I had to wear that stupid tartan suit. She replied, 'If you were going to see the queen, you'd dress up, wouldn't you?' It was hard to disagree. 'Well,' she continued, 'you're going to see the King of Kings!' The problem was that even as a child I could see the flaw in my mother's argument. If God was who he claimed to be, then he was everywhere — not just shut up in a stuffy old church building. Therefore, he didn't see me just in my suit; he saw me all the time — whether I was dressed in smart clothes,

scruffy clothes or no clothes at all. I was forced to conclude
that it wasn't God I was wearing the suit for; it was all of the
other people at the service. But those clothes gave a completely
false impression of who I really was. So I learnt at an early age
that going to church was synonymous with pretending to be
something that I was not.

If I can't be me in the context of church—if I can't ask my
deepest questions, express my deepest fears—my soul cannot
be fed there. If I can't be me in the context of church—if I
can't raise my doubts, let my hair down, chill out, drop my
guard—where else can I do this? The place where our deepest needs are met will become our home. Home is where you
don't have to pretend. Human beings are made for community,
and communities that are worth belonging to are honest.

ASK NO QUESTIONS

Many of us aren't good at dealing with mess. We like things
to be cut and dried. We like to know just where we stand—a
confident faith built on sound doctrine. This is, of course, a
great strength: it guards against the dilution and erosion of our
identity. It makes us distinctive. But on the shadow side of every
strength is a weakness. And our weakness is that we've tended
to put so much value on theological soundness that we've lost
the ability to handle mess and doubt. As a result, all too often
we respond to people's sincere problems and crises of faith not
by reaching out to help them slowly work through the issues
but by expecting them just to snap out of it. Sometimes it can
even seem that we're interested in having a conversation only
if we know all the answers in advance.

A few years ago I read an account by a man who had, after
years of unhappiness, left his church altogether. His article
explained why he had taken this step and finished with a conclusion that has stayed with me ever since and is certain to be
on my mind for years to come. It simply read: 'In the end, I'm

happier to live with questions I cannot answer than with questions I cannot ask.'

Nigel Wright warns in his book *The Radical Evangelical*, 'Large numbers of liberals are refugee fundamentalists.' If someone doesn't feel able to sign on the dotted line, we tend to view them with suspicion, if not outright hostility. Rather than teasing out what the problem is and going on to think it through with them—humbly and on an equal footing—we tend to assert through our body language, and even our words, that their faith or worldview must be defective. And to those on the receiving end, this can feel a bit like a shape-up-or-ship-out attitude. Though occasionally we do this explicitly, in truth it's more often something we do unconsciously to those who dare to voice any kind of doubt or uncertainty.

The harsh realities of a hard-line, intolerant approach—which we are all quick to condemn in others but slow to perceive in ourselves—are powerfully shown by Fyodor Dostoevsky in his great novel *The Brothers Karamazov*, the story of three brothers torn apart by guilt after the murder of their father. In the best-known chapter, atheist intellectual Ivan tells younger brother Alyosha that he's dreamt about Jesus' return. Making it clear this isn't the second coming, Ivan explains that the return takes place in sixteenth-century Seville during the time of the infamous Spanish Inquisition.

Appearing with no fanfare, Jesus travels on foot to Seville Cathedral and promptly finds himself being arrested by the ninety-year-old cardinal grand inquisitor. The inquisitor visits Jesus in prison, calmly telling him he'll be burned at the stake the next day. Jesus says nothing as the old man details the charge against him. He'll be killed, the inquisitor explains, because he jeopardizes people's salvation. He gives them too much freedom. People may all have been born with freedom, the inquisitor goes on, but only a tiny elite actually have the moral strength and courage to cope with it—to handle the complexities of distinguishing right from wrong and to believe in the face of doubt and uncertainty. The majority of folk just aren't up to the demands of the task.

'I tell you,' the grand inquisitor continues, 'humans are pathetic creatures, with no more urgent need than to find someone to whom they can surrender the gift of freedom they were born with.' This, he explains, is what Jesus failed to understand the first time. By refusing to give in to the temptation in the wilderness of throwing himself off the top of the temple, or to come down from the cross — actions that would have proved his power and identity beyond all doubt — he saddled people with the crippling burden of having to think for themselves. 'We've corrected your mighty achievement,' the old man boasts, defending the brutal way in which the Inquisition forces people to believe the church's doctrines. 'They'll accept whatever we tell them with joy, because they'll have been spared the anguish and torment of having to make their own, free and independent choices.'

This is the terrible danger we face. Like the inquisitor in Ivan's dream, we crave certainty. We want things to be absolutely beyond doubt — black or white, right or wrong. We want science to give us clear-cut, objective facts. We want the Bible to supply us with neat and easily digestible answers to all our questions. And we want preachers to feed us with the pure, unadulterated, prepackaged Word of God. We want guaranteed answers. We want shoot-from-the-hip certainty. We don't want to have to think, agonize or grapple with life's difficult questions.

Too many of the evangelistic presentations I have heard over the years have fallen into the trap of telling potential converts that all their problems, all their cares and concerns, will be lifted if they allow Jesus into their lives. Just the other day I heard an evangelist speaking to a busy street of shoppers in London. 'You're all miserable,' he told them. 'If materialism was making you happy you'd all be smiling, but I can't see any of you smiling.' He went on to tell the crowd that if they'd just turn to the Saviour, they would never know sadness again.

I'm deeply uncomfortable with this seriously dishonest misinterpretation or distortion of the gospel—and so, I could see, were the rest of his audience.

JESUS LET PEOPLE DOUBT

In all four gospels, Jesus' disciples are shown making mistake after mistake—alternating between intense faith and crippling doubt, great insight and gobsmacking stupidity. But how did Jesus respond? Far from cracking down hard, he gave them space; he never demanded absolute certainty or doctrinal orthodoxy from them. Instead he gently worked with them, listening to their doubts, coaching and mentoring them through their temptations, fears and misunderstandings, leading them to a place of strength.

Jesus doesn't give us certainty. Instead he invites us to have *faith*. And that's very different. He accepted that even his closest and most loyal followers (the church's future leaders) would have their doubts and their misunderstandings. But rather than adopting a policy of zero tolerance, he encouraged them to *explore* their doubts to deepen their faith.

Jesus didn't come to make people superhuman but to help them be fully human. His message was one designed to help us to cope with life—to help them deal with pressure, guilt, failure, pain, hopes and dreams—not to take away all our cares by magic. God is with us in our pain, but he doesn't remove it—no more evidence is needed than Psalm 22, which Jesus quotes on the cross. Writing to the church in Rome, Paul encourages his friends this way:

> Who shall separate us from the love of Christ? Shall trouble or hardship or persecution or famine or nakedness or danger or sword? ...

I am convinced that neither death nor life, neither angels
nor demons, neither the present nor the future, nor any powers,
neither height nor depth, nor anything else in all creation, will
be able to separate us from the love of God that is in Christ
Jesus our Lord.

(Romans 8:35, 38–39)

While Paul clearly teaches that we are to 'pray in the Spirit
on all occasions' (Ephesians 6:18), he obviously assumes that
trouble, hardship, persecution, famine, nakedness, danger, sword
and death not only can, but do happen to Christians.

An honest gospel is not a denial of the pains and pressures of
life. Instead our focus should be opening a conversation about
faith that takes questions, doubt, pain and struggle seriously.
Jesus may have said that 'the truth will set you free' (John 8:32),
but he never said that freedom wouldn't hurt. If our mission is
to bring life in all its fullness, then we need to begin with the
honesty of Christ.

'If a man will begin with certainties, he shall end in doubts,'
wrote Francis Bacon, 'but if he will be content to begin with
doubts, he shall end in certainties.' From the temptation to
throw himself from the highest point of the temple in plain
view of the crowds (Matthew 4:5–6), to the constant demands
for him to produce a sign to prove who he was, to the final
taunts for him to come down from the cross, Jesus consistently
refused to do things that would provide certainties and force
people into believing in him. He always allowed room for
doubt but presented people with the opportunity to deepen
their faith through exploring it.

Jesus never pushed, forced, bludgeoned, beat, coerced,
cajoled, manhandled or manipulated people into faith—he
never threatened them with the kind of offer they couldn't
refuse. In contrast to the high-handed interventionist approach
we so often adopt, his efforts to bring the people he encountered into a closer relationship with God were characterized by

what Philip Yancey calls 'the slow, steady undertow of grace'.
He had what we often lack—the maturity to see that faith isn't
something you either have or don't have but rather something
that develops slowly over the course of a lifetime from small
to big, from shallow to profound, as we grow in our relationship with God. As Scots theologian Robert Davidson puts it,
'Faith does not depend on our grasp of God, but on God's
grasp of us.'

Jesus responded to his people's doubt by offering them
something—or more particularly someone—to believe in.
When a father brought his demon-possessed son to him for
healing, the man begged, 'If you can do anything, take pity
on us and help us' (Mark 9:22). The disciples had already
tried—and failed—to exorcise the boy themselves, which
must have dented the father's initial confidence in bringing him
to Jesus. But rather than rebuking him for his lack of faith—'I
do believe; help me overcome my unbelief!'—Jesus healed the
boy there and then. He didn't wait for the father's faith to be
100 percent or anything near it.

In the same way, rather than rebuking Thomas for his doubts
about the resurrection, Jesus invited him to deepen his faith:
'Put your finger here; see my hands. Reach out your hand and
put it into my side. Stop doubting and believe' (John 20:27).
And for those who are tempted to hear in these words a tone of
impatience and frustration—of *demand* rather than *gentle invitation*—it's worth noticing that the encouragement for Thomas
not to doubt comes *after* the invitation to explore these doubts
for himself with the kind of in-depth probing (literally putting
his hands into Jesus' wounds) most of us would find deeply dis-
respectful. In fact, Jesus was prepared to give Thomas far more
space than he needed—but it seems Thomas never did take
Jesus up on his offer. A rebuke might have pulled Thomas into
line, but an invitation to explore his doubt deepened his faith
considerably. As F. F. Bruce put it, 'Thomas might have been

slower than his fellow-disciples to come to faith in the risen
Christ, but when he did so, his faith was expressed in language
which went beyond any that they had used: "My Lord and my
God!'"

Jesus invites but never compels us to believe. As a result,
we'd do well to avoid making snap judgements about whether
someone is in or out of the Christian community based on his
ability to sign up to this or that established statement of faith.
Instead we should learn how to create the opportunities for
the unchurched to gradually deepen their faith and relationship with God. Questioning and doubt do not put real faith
in jeopardy. Faith isn't certainty. It's a risky commitment to a
glimpsed possibility in the face of reasonable human hesitation
about whether it is really possible. We're so keen for things to
be cut and dried, we often fail to see that faith and doubt aren't
mutually exclusive. As the German-born theologian Paul Tillich wrote, 'Doubt isn't the opposite of faith. It is an element
of faith.' Where there's absolute certainty, there can be no room
for faith.

JESUS' HUMANITY

An interesting transition has taken place over the church's
two-thousand-year history. The early church frequently struggled with the question, 'Was Jesus really God?' For the first
believers, Jesus' humanity was rarely questioned—it was self-
evident. They knew he was a man—many of them had laughed,
cried, talked and eaten with him. That Jesus was God, however,
was a much more significant mental hurdle.

When John, in his first letter, wrote, 'That which was
from the beginning, which we have heard, which we have
seen with our eyes, which we have looked at and our hands
have touched—this we proclaim concerning the Word of life'
(1 John 1:1), he knew it was a remarkable statement. For John
and the other disciples to reach the point where they firmly and

unshakably believed that their friend and teacher was divine was the result of a long and challenging journey.

Today, however, we find it much harder to believe that Jesus was genuinely and fully human—in fact many Christians still find the thought somewhat offensive.

As our distance in time from the events of the first century AD has increased, so has our doubt regarding Jesus' humanity. Centuries of stained-glass windows depicting him with a halo on his head and an angelic, otherworldly expression on his face serve only to reinforce our error. We will fight to defend Christ's divinity but struggle with, and are sometimes downright embarrassed by, the implications of his humanity. What was Jesus doing on his eighteenth birthday? Who was his best friend? His special aunt? Which girls did he fancy? What was his favourite drink? His funniest joke? His greatest temptation? How did he spend the long summer evenings through his twenties? What games did he play? What songs did he whistle or hum as he worked?

Jesus was human in the fullest possible sense. He experienced hunger, thirst, pain, sorrow, tiredness, joy, pressure, tension, rejection, fear, anger—the full gamut of human feelings, needs and emotions. He attended to all of the functions associated with physicality—the consequences of eating and drinking were no less real for Jesus than for you and me.

Furthermore Jesus was tempted by self-centeredness in exactly the same way we are. Two famous examples of this are his forty-day fast (where, in the wilderness, he was tempted by Satan to feed himself, to test his divinity and to achieve great wealth and power) and the garden of Gethsemane (where he spent a long night battling with his desire to walk away from what awaited him). Because of what the Bible tells us about Jesus' humanity, we know that these were just two moments in a continuous struggle to live the life he was called to rather than taking the easy, self-centred option.

The fourth-century church leader Gregory of Nazianzus (AD 325–389), one of the Desert Fathers, understood the theological importance of Jesus' absolute humanity. In one of the most profound statements ever made about the nature of atonement, he taught that 'what is not assumed cannot be redeemed'. His point was this: if Jesus had not entered into the human experience fully, he could not have secured the redemption of humanity.

In 1988, cinemas around the world were picketed by thousands of evangelical Christians. The film they rallied against was Martin Scorsese's *The Last Temptation of Christ* based on Nikos Kazantzakis's 1955 novel of the same name. The film, an obviously fictional take on the gospel stories, depicts a very human Jesus who struggles with doubt and temptation. In one scene, while hanging on the cross, Jesus pictures himself in a sexual relationship with Mary Magdalene. This scene caused the most controversy and inspired people to protest outside cinemas showing the film. It was considered blasphemy to suggest that Jesus was tempted sexually and heresy to suppose that it was not easy for him to resist any temptation he faced. The great irony is that the problem with Scorsese's film was not theological but psychological. Jesus would have been tempted sexually, but not, our own humanity reliably tells us, in the midst of enduring the utter pain and humiliation of death on a cross.

The critics of *The Last Temptation of Christ* perhaps did not understand the importance and power of Gregory's words or of the New Testament's own verdict. 'For we do not have a high priest who is unable to sympathize with our weaknesses, but we have one who has been tempted in every way, just as we are—yet was without sin' (Hebrews 4:15). Were Jesus not tempted sexually he would not have been fully human; what is more, he would have no power to redeem us from our failings in that area. Had Jesus not been tempted in all areas—and resisted—he would not have absolutely triumphed over sin.

If the real reason he overcame temptation was that his divinity protected him and he could, therefore, have easily gone forty, four hundred or even four thousand days without food or water in the desert had he chosen to, then his example offers no hope and little inspiration for us in our struggle to live the life God chooses for us.

We also see Jesus' humanity revealed in his teaching. He was a practical teacher who addressed the issues that his listeners wanted to know about on a level they could relate to. Rather than talking in the lofty terms and phraseology of academics and scholars, he told stories of everyday life—stories of sheep and goats, coins and seeds. He spoke in a language that his audience could readily understand and relate to. Spending time with Jesus must have been a refreshing break from a world filled with pious religiosity and pomposity. His message was accessible, straightforward, relevant and, most important, honest—it made sense and offered real hope instead of creating unrealistic burdens. Jesus never claimed that following him would be easy—just that what he said was true.

Watchman Nee, the famous Chinese Christian leader, explained in his classic book *The Normal Christian Life* that rather than enjoying a superhuman or super-spiritual life, as we have so often been led to believe, Jesus simply lived a whole and normal life. Indeed, he was the only person ever to live a fully human life, as God intended human life to be. We on the other hand, because of our self-centeredness, end up leading subnormal existences. Christ simply calls us to follow him into normality.

Paul's teaching that Jesus was the second Adam (Romans 5:12–20) reflects this perspective. Where Adam, the first human, succumbed to temptation, Jesus stood firm. Where Adam caved in to sin, Jesus refused to surrender. But it was as a human being that Jesus overcame temptation. It was as a human being that he obeyed his Father. It was as a human being that he suffered, cared, wept, slept, served, struggled with his fears and doubts—and overcame. That Jesus was 100 percent human while simultaneously being one hundred percent God is the truth that offers us real hope. As the second Adam, Jesus sets out an example to which we all can aspire. It is precisely the honesty and earthiness of the incarnation that moves us, challenges us and encourages us. We worship and serve the God of the Bible precisely because he became one of us.

THE CHURCH'S RESPONSE

Our task, both as individuals made in his image and together as the community of the church, is simply to mirror God, to reflect him honestly and authentically. Thus, first, our message is that whoever you are, whatever you are struggling with, whatever your doubts, questions and temptations, God understands the difficulties you are facing and has faced them himself. Then we go on to say that we struggle too, that we don't have all the answers. Life is also a battle for us. We have fears and insecurities, temptations and unanswered questions.

The challenge, as Rudyard Kipling famously put it, is to 'trust yourself when all men doubt you, but make allowance for their doubting too.' The problem is that in reality most of us feel threatened by those whose views are different from ours, and we tend to act as if the weakness is theirs, chastising them for their error of judgement or lack of faith. When our faith isn't robust enough to deal with ambiguity and uncertainty, we become insecure, shying away from those with different views, insisting on strict party lines. A strong church, like a strong person, can afford to be gentle, thoughtful and restrained. It can afford to extend a helping hand to others. It is a weak church that lacks confidence, that blusters or acts aggressively.

Honest churches must begin where people are, not where we assume they are or would like them to be. We must discover where they are by listening with humility and compassion.

Perhaps the greatest challenge for us is to accept that being an honest church means that we will not try to give people all the answers. We will somehow allow people room to struggle, to grieve, to doubt, to question, to develop at their own speed without being cajoled or manipulated. The church that stands on the edge of its community and shouts at it will not work—it never has worked. It never will work.

If we are to create honest churches we must provide environments in which questions can be freely asked and in which teaching actually relates to the realities of people's lives. We should not ignore the hard, down-to-earth topics (for example, money, sexuality, doubt, fear, temptation and suffering), beginning with practical principles for life rather than detached doctrines. And we should listen at least as much as we talk.

Missiologist Lesslie Newbigin said, 'We do not seek to impose our Christian beliefs upon others, but this is not because (as in the liberal view) we recognise that they may be right and we may be wrong. It is because the Christian faith itself, centred in the message of the incarnation, cross and resurrection, forbids the use of any kind of coercive pressure upon others to conform.'

We use the term *tolerance* a great deal in our culture; but we do so in a much diluted form. The dictionary definition is 'the quality of accepting other people's rights to their own opinions, beliefs and actions'. To tolerate is to treat someone with generosity. However, these definitions do not imply agreement. The only people who can be truly tolerant are those who are confident in what they believe but secure enough to leave space for others to choose their own way.

Paul's prayer should be ours too: 'And pray for us, too, that God may open a door for our message, so that we may proclaim the mystery of Christ, for which I am in chains. Pray that I may proclaim it clearly, as I should. Be wise in the way you act toward outsiders; make the most of every opportunity'

(Colossians 4:3–5). An honest church community will be one that strives to make people feel comfortable to be who they really are.

Awhile ago a friend of mine, as part of his masters degree, undertook a piece of research on a number of large churches from different denominations and church traditions (charismatic and noncharismatic, evangelical and mainline, Protestant and Catholic, and so on), all of which were experiencing periods of growth. His task was to identify the common threads that accounted for their growth. After a year's work, he reached his conclusion. The one thing they had in common was this — each was a community where people laughed together. He realised that this was because each church provided the kind of environment in which people were relaxed enough to be able to laugh. You only really laugh when you can be yourself — when you feel comfortable.

An intelligent church is an honest church.

YES, BUT HOW?

What does an honest church look like? It's a hard question but a vital one if we want to be authentic. Authenticity would make our songs address life's lows as well as highs, laments as well as celebrations — like the Psalms. Our teaching would be more grounded. Our leadership would be more vulnerable. Our mission would be more integrated. Our discipleship would be more about journeying than arriving.

○   ○   ○

QUESTIONS

1. Begin to model honesty. When people ask you how you are, make a conscious effort to tell them the real answer (without crossing boundaries). When you ask others how they are, really listen to what they have to say. Do

not allow yourself to jump in with all the answers. Just listen, and promise to pray for that person. If you can be the answer to that prayer, then do it—but sensitively and wisely.

2. Experiment with different forms of response in services. Allow people to think in silence, to be vulnerable before God and to respond to him in different ways than you normally do. By doing so, you encourage more thoughtful reflection and honest response.

3. Explore ways of using your building or resources to serve the community. You will need to make a list of principles so that the use of the building reflects your values. Are there some groups in the community that could use the building at a reduced rate? A good place to start is with residents associations, neighbourhood watches, self-help groups and other voluntary groups. Let these groups know you want to help them. Start the conversation.

4. Make a list of the big issues your community is facing—it might be debt, family, addiction, stress, crime or education. Once you have made the list, see if you can pull together a team to work on material that can be used in services and small groups to help people explore these issues. If you have folk in the church who do not normally preach or teach but are specialists in these areas, get them involved. Allow people to be honest about their own struggles as you prepare this material—using real stories to let people know that these are issues that most people struggle with.

5. As a church leader, be honest yourself. What are the pressures you are trying to cover up or hide away? Don't be too proud to be open with your leadership

team, with the wider church leadership in the town or with your congregation. Let people know how they can pray for you, and seek advice on the issues you need help with. Model honesty, and people will be honest with you.

CHAPTER 5

PURPOSEFUL
CHURCH

An intelligent church is a purposeful church. A purposeful church is one that is intentional and strategically
aware—one that has clear goals, objectives, targets and outcomes.

ANTI-STRATEGY

For some, the whole idea of strategic planning and structural
development feels wrong—it is, they say, unspiritual. For them,
church strategy is an oxymoron—you rely either on God or
on your own ideas. They are far happier with the concept of
organic and relational development. Their concern is that we
don't sell out to the secular management gurus by adopting
techniques that, although fine in the workplace, should not be
used in churches because they shut the door on God's Spirit.
Ironically, regarding planning as a limitation on God's power is
itself imposing limits upon him.

These kinds of sentiments link two very different groups.
Over the years I have constantly heard the worries of those
who would term themselves *traditionalists* around this area; but
more recently I've heard exactly the same concerns from some
emerging churchers.

Another reason churches don't plan is that they see it as being time-consuming and difficult. And, of course, they are right. Planning does soak up time and take enormous effort. However, no matter how tough the demands of planning may be, the struggles it involves pale into insignificance compared to the difficulties of trying to live and work without it. Having strategic goals and objectives is the most efficient and effective route to getting any job done and done well.

Imagine opening a box of flat-pack furniture only to discover that the instructions for its assembly have not been included. The pile of fibreboard and bags of screws, bolts and doweling pieces scattered across your floor could be a bookcase or a chest of drawers; without a plan for its construction and an idea of what it's supposed to look like, it is not likely to become anything. Having a plan not only makes a job easier; sometimes it makes the difference between effective and impossible.

Sheer impatience makes people reticent to plan. 'Let's stop the talking and just get on with it!' they say. They do not realise that time well spent in planning is not wasted; it actually reduces the amount of time and effort needed to succeed in achieving a project.

Ten minutes spent at home writing a shopping list could be seen as a way of putting off the arduous trek to the supermarket. In reality, the planning process makes the whole shopping trip much easier and faster. Rather than wandering aimlessly up and down every aisle trying to make decisions on the run, the shopper can simply hunt down the items on the list. A list takes all of the guesswork out of the process and also produces a cheaper basket of goods at the checkout counter. Of course, a shopping list is not a rigid document — it still allows for the shopper to take advantage of special offers (being opportunistic) or to buy unplanned items (being led by inspiration). But a list serves as a guide, ensuring that items are not forgotten or duplicated.

GOD PLANS

God himself is a strategist and a long-distance planner—it is part of his nature. At the beginning of his letter to the Ephesians, the apostle Paul makes it clear that God had chosen them before the creation of the world. In fact the whole of the letter is littered with references to God's planning. Here's just one example: 'For we are God's workmanship, created in Christ Jesus to do good works, which God prepared in advance for us to do' (Ephesians 2:10).

Not only did Paul understand something of God's strategic nature and approach; he sought to mirror it in his own life. Paul's overarching strategic goal was to reach Rome and preach the gospel there (see Romans 1:13). His planning simply echoes the fact that God is a planner—planning is written into creation; we are all made in the image of the God who purposefully plans.

One of the most famous verses in the Bible speaks clearly of God's purposeful mission. 'For God so loved the world that he gave his one and only Son, that whoever believes in him shall not perish but have eternal life' (John 3:16). The passage is pregnant with purpose. John's simple summation of the gospel doesn't solely concern the *what* of Christ's life and death but also the *why*. God did not send his Son on the off chance that it would change things for the better. The incarnation was a decisive and purposeful act—one, Scripture is clear, God had preordained and planned with a specific objective in mind.

Jesus' life was similarly purposeful. His mission took place over the course of an action-packed three-year period. He proactively sought a new world order. As we see in John's gospel, Jesus had a definite sense of timing and priority. For instance, when Jesus' brothers told him he should go to Jerusalem so that people could see his miracles, he told them, 'The right time for me has not yet come; for you any time is right. The world cannot hate you, but it hates me because I testify that what it does is evil. You go to the Feast. I am not yet going up to this Feast, because for me the right time has not yet come' (John 7:6–8). He knew that entering the capital city would provoke a showdown with the Jewish establishment that would end in his death—which he did not wish to initiate until the right moment.

After three years of hard work, that moment arrived. He knew the exact time to take on the authorities. Jesus had taught and trained his disciples. He'd mentored them in an understanding of the principles of the kingdom of God. Now was the moment for him to challenge the power of the state full on. Thus, he chose to provoke his enemies through an intentionally confrontational course of action: he presented himself as king. Jesus' decision to ride into Jerusalem on the back of a donkey is popularly portrayed as one of extraordinary humility. But that is only half the story. It was also a premeditated act of rebellion and revolution. Riding into a city on horseback was traditionally and symbolically something that only a conquering king would do. Riding a donkey may not seem grand, but Jesus—and the Jewish authorities—knew that by doing so, he was making a public declaration of his claim to the status of Messiah—in fulfilment of an ancient prophecy (Zechariah 9:9).

Jesus was nothing if not in control. His actions were designed deliberately to telegraph a message to both friends and enemies alike.

LEADERSHIP

The church's task is simply to echo God. And that means purposeful and strategic mission must be at its core so that it may prove itself effective. A purposeful mission might take many forms, but it will necessarily be intentional and intentionally led. Genuine vision must clothe itself in strategic planning. Indeed, this is what marks it apart from the simple act of dreaming. Real vision has an inbuilt and natural inclination or impulse to plan and lead.

To take an example from the Old Testament: For four hundred years, while serving as slaves in Egypt, the people of Israel had dreamt of freedom. But it wasn't until Moses, prodded by God, reluctantly but effectively stepped forward to lead them that they were eventually able to shake off the chains of slavery.

Just a few months ago a good friend who is an emerging church disciple recommended a book to me titled *The Myth of Leadership*. Too much talk of leadership makes people nervous. But is such a stance biblical? To turn our backs on the process of leadership, strategic planning and goal setting is to fall into a trap that has dogged the church for centuries— dualism. The division of the sacred from the secular, of faith from fact, of science from religion is, and always has been, a mistake. In reality no separation exists between them.

GOALS

Goals and objectives are the practical way in which any vision is translated into reality. Simply put, a goal is something you want to achieve—a place you are headed—and objectives are the smaller steps you will take in order to attain that goal.

Before you set out on any journey it helps to know three things: first, where you are now—your starting point; second, where you want to end up— your destination; and third, how you are going to get there—your route. The more you know about your starting point and destination the easier it is to work out your route. However, to set off for a destination without having researched your route and considered whether you have enough resources for the journey is at best foolish and at worst disastrous.

To repeat Tom Peters' advice, 'Always start with the end in mind.' It is your final goal that needs to be settled first. Where do you want to be in three, five or ten years? It is your task to define the precise nature of your goal (or set of goals) as clearly as possible. What do you want to achieve? Where do you want to go? How will you know when you get there? Unless you are clear about where you are heading, you will never be able to direct others well—plus you'll waste a great deal of your own time going round in circles. Or, to quote Lewis Carol, 'if you don't know where you're going, you'll end up somewhere else.'

I've been consulting churches for years. Here's what I've learnt: those who don't set goals (either because they think they can't or simply won't) always decline. No matter how strong or spiritual they think they are, or give off the air of being, without intention and direction they are like an untethered boat—when the weather's calm everything looks fine, but when a storm sets in (as it always does) they are adrift, tossed and turned by every wave and gust of wind.

Church.co.uk, Waterloo, has three goals. We strive to be the following:

24/7—providing a welcome to everyone whatever their situation, whatever the time, night or day.

Holistic—offering a breadth and depth of support, spiritually and socially to our surrounding community and beyond.

Global—working to develop our impact both nationally and internationally.

It is against these three goals that we constantly measure everything we do. And everything we do is prompted by these three goals, even the writing of this book.

OBJECTIVES

Once you've defined your goals, it's essential to break them down into a number of smaller, more measurable objectives, or practical steps, through which you will achieve them and by which you will be able to easily monitor your progress or lack of it. Set them firmly, but at the same time keep them flexible. Just as a closed road might force you to change your route, so circumstances may necessitate a changed approach to your plan.

Whatever your goal, the only way to get there is one step at a time. As they say, the only way to move a mountain is one pebble at a time. If your goal was to build a shed, you might break that task down into four smaller objectives: First, find a do-it-yourself book. Second, buy some wood and nails. Third, invite a friend over to help. Fourth, make coffee while he builds. Job complete. Mission accomplished. Goal reached.

Of course, the complexity of your objectives depends on the nature of your goal. You may need to break them down again into a series of even more specific timed and manageable tasks. (For example, 'Find a do-it-yourself book' becomes 'Surf the Internet, decide on the best book for your needs, order the book, read the book.')

It's also important, and natural, to give your most detailed thought to crossing the ground immediately ahead of you, since this is always what you can see most clearly and must navigate most urgently. 'The Devil is in the detail' no matter how grand the plan. Whatever the project, the greatest risk to its success will be at the level of seemingly tiny details. Areas of weakness and woolly thinking will be exposed only by working hard to identify each objective and its component parts (or tasks) and then timetabling it against the name of a specific individual or team.

You should be able to answer four questions about any objective and task you have set yourself.

What? Be specific. Each objective/task should be big enough to present a challenge but also realistic enough to attain. If objectives are set too high or too low, they will fail to inspire much enthusiasm.

How? You need a clear plan for achieving each objective/task. What resources (money, time, talents, space) are needed to attain the desired result? Be honest—it hurts, but it's the only way to make progress.

Who? It doesn't matter how many people you have involved in the delivery of an objective/task but rather whose name is in the frame in terms of final responsibility. At this point you need the name of a specific individual with whom the buck stops.

When? You need ambitious but realistic deadlines for when each of your objectives/tasks should be completed. 'As soon as possible' usually means 'when I can get around to it'—which is an infinitely postponable date. Deadlines allow for accountability.

WHEN PLANS GO AWRY

Plans evolve, objectives slip, circumstances change, mistakes get made, visions fail. I could fill a very long book with the list of failed and changed plans from the history of Oasis and Church.co.uk. That's why the ability to adapt and improvise is so important to any leader. But when your plans don't work out as first envisioned, take time to reflect on how and why they failed. You can learn as much from your failures as successes. If your objectives/tasks are not being achieved, you should ask the following questions of yourself and your team: What can we learn from this for the future? What problems did we ignore or underestimate? Were the reasons for our failure inside or outside our control? How can we overcome this problem? Could we have foreseen the problem? How can we revise our objective or change our plan?

Remember that objectives and tasks are just the means to an end, not the end itself. It's OK to adjust them as you develop your direction and review your progress. It is important to never lose sight of your goal but, just as on any journey, remember that a number of different routes to get somewhere can be found. The apostle Paul suffered many setbacks in terms of his goal to visit the church in Rome and preach in the city (Romans 1:11–13). However, he refused to let go of this goal and thus saw each setback as another opportunity to reassess his progress before developing a revised plan for the way forward.

Awhile ago I was able to meet the Brazilian football legend, Pele. I will always remember one conversation I had with him. I asked him what he thought was the most important lesson he had learnt over his years of playing football at every level. His response was fascinating. He told me he had played football all over the world and had listened to literally thousands of team talks. These locker-room instructions had varied widely in terms of tactics, but they were all exactly the same in one regard — they all told the team what to do but completely ignored the fact that the other team on the field could wreck all plans within moments of kickoff. The greatest lesson Pele ever learnt in football was simply this: winning is all about restarting from a position you never expected to be in.

An intelligent church is a purposeful church.

YES, BUT HOW?

A purposeful church is one that remains outcome focused. The Victorian gentry had a curious habit of building follies — structures with no obvious purpose or function, building for building's sake. The saga of the UK's ill-fated Millennium Dome (built at the cost of more than one hundred million pounds on the south bank of the river Thames in London, to celebrate the new millennium; the Dome was massively over-budget and, despite being an impressive structure, has been left unoccupied since 2001) suggests that the art of folly building survives today.

Our church buildings and programmes should not fall into the same trap — if nothing else, it's a matter of good stewardship.

The good news is that as long as the purpose of the church is clear and the planning motivated and measured against stated goals, we won't fall into the trap. Put another way, our goals must shape our projects, meetings and/or timetable rather than the other way round.

○ ○ ○

QUESTIONS

1. Ask your congregation why they think the church is in the community it is in. Record their answers. Ask them what they think the church's vision and purpose are. Do the same with the church leadership. Work out where God has placed your particular congregation.

2. Ask the community what they think the church is there for and what they think the church could do to help and serve the community.

3. Look at the history of your church — what has it stood for, what are its values, where is it going? This whole process could take a year, but it is well worth it. As you pull all the answers together, begin to plan for what you are going to do as a church to engage with your community, with wider society and with the world. Make a simple list of things you can do, and get teams together to see it through.

4. Proactively connect attendees and community organisations. Don't personally try to be the answer to everyone's needs; instead help people to work out how they can use the gifts, skills and personalities God has given them to best serve him and each other. Look for some good small group material that can help people discover their purpose. Think about booking an 'intelligent church weekend' to help you do this.

5. Once you have outlined the purpose of the church, make sure you regularly communicate it with the congregation and the community. Nehemiah communicated his vision every twenty-eight days. Make sure your vision and purpose statements are simple, straightforward and easy to understand. Then make sure that you constantly ask whether what you are doing fits that vision and purpose. Don't be afraid to stop some programmes and activities if they no longer fit the vision and purpose of the church.

CHAPTER 6

GENEROUS
CHURCH

An intelligent church is a generous church. Generosity is defined as the act of giving or sharing more than is necessary or expected. Jesus was clear: 'Give,' he instructed his followers, 'a good measure, pressed down, shaken together and running over' (Luke 6:38). The people who encounter us should get more—much more—than they expected, needed, bargained for or ever thought possible.

GOD GIVES

We must never stray far from the truth that God, in his generous love, primarily defines and identifies all humanity as good—made in his image. And he offers his rich blessings to all.

I love the slogan of the United Kingdom charity Christian Aid: 'We believe in life before death.' What a wonderful way of summing up a major part of Jesus' message, an echo of the central emphasis of his revolutionary ministry. The weak will be strong and the poor will be rich. Jesus' claim was simple: God was far more generous than the religious leaders who had been responsible for representing him. His inaugural address, the Sermon on the Mount, announced the arrival of the kingdom of God and the breaking in of shalom—spiritual, physical,

emotional and social well-being—for all, bar none, except by
his or her own decision. It was a message that was shot through
with hope, liberation and God's generosity.

Jesus granted worth and dignity to those who for so long
had been deprived of it. He forgave, healed and restored the
humanity of thousands who had given up on themselves simply because society, led by the religious institutions of the day,
had given up on them. His three years of ministry were spent
undermining unjust social systems and setting about the down-
fall of religious intolerance. This is the gospel of Jesus Christ,
and nothing less is. God's generosity is available right here, right
now, to all through Jesus.

As Jesus himself put it:

> The Spirit of the Lord is on me,
>   because he has anointed me
>   to preach good news to the poor.
> He has sent me to proclaim freedom for the prisoners
>   and recovery of sight for the blind, to release the
>   oppressed,
>   to proclaim the year of the Lord's favour.
>
>   (Luke 4:18–19)

Our manifesto is the same—to proclaim God's favour
through our generosity. Jesus constantly modelled this right-
here, right-now message. He was not so much a preacher concerned with the way things could be as an activist concerned
with the way things actually were. He didn't so much practice
what he preached as preach what he practiced. Not only did he
show extraordinary patience with his twelve closest followers,
but others too received his full and generous attention. Let's
consider more closely the story of Zacchaeus which I have
already mentioned earlier.

> Jesus entered Jericho and was passing through. A man was
> there by the name of Zacchaeus; he was a chief tax collector

and was wealthy. He wanted to see who Jesus was, but being a short man he could not, because of the crowd. So he ran ahead and climbed a sycamore-fig tree to see him, since Jesus was coming that way.

When Jesus reached the spot, he looked up and said to him, 'Zacchaeus, come down immediately. I must stay at your house today.' So he came down at once and welcomed him gladly.

All the people saw this and began to mutter, 'He has gone to be the guest of a "sinner".'

But Zacchaeus stood up and said to the Lord, 'Look, Lord! Here and now I give half of my possessions to the poor, and if I have cheated anybody out of anything, I will pay back four times the amount.'

Jesus said to him, 'Today salvation has come to this house, because this man, too, is a son of Abraham. For the Son of Man came to seek and to save what was lost.'

(Luke 19:1 – 10)

It's interesting to note that Zacchaeus, like so many of the other people who Jesus singled out and gave his time to, was altogether the wrong kind of person for a respectable and religious Jew to be involved with. Of the entire crowd there on that day, Zacchaeus was probably the person most readily (and publicly) labeled as a sinner.

Sin in the days of the New Testament was sticky — if you spent time with sinners, you too would end up dirty. For this reason Jesus was labeled a sinner himself by some of the Jews in John 9:18 – 25. But Jesus believed the opposite; as far as he was concerned grace and generosity were sticky, not sin. The sinners and the outcasts, those previously pushed to the fringes of society, were no longer the 'wrong' people; instead they were the very people he was looking for.

When a person fails morally we often comment that they fell from grace. Jesus would fundamentally disagree — his life, actions and teaching all demonstrate the opposite. With him we don't fall from grace, we fall into grace.

WE NEED TO COPY GOD

The brilliant mathematician and philosopher Blaise Pascal once explained, 'We are all made in the image of the God we choose to serve.' Or, to quote Anton Chekhov, 'man is what he believes.' Our first thought of God fundamentally shapes both us and our message. If our understanding of God is that his first impulse for humanity is outrageous love, then we too will slowly learn to respond with that same love (albeit a limited and broken replica of the real thing). If we believe God responds to us primarily in anger or rejection, we too will mimic this trait.

If we are truly to bring good news to the world, we cannot begin by despising its citizens. Our task is to demonstrate the unconditional love of God to all people — his shalom — regardless of their gender, marital status, race, ethnicity, religion, age, sexual orientation, social status or intellectual ability. If we truly believe that we were made in God's image, created with original goodness but marred by sin, and that God in his generosity demonstrated his love for us and saved us 'while we were still sinners' (Romans 5:8), we will be compelled to imitate him.

GENEROUS WITH OUR RESOURCES

It is wisely said that the character of a person is revealed by the way in which he treats those from whom he has nothing to gain. What better way to live this out than by sharing our money with the poor, with those who can never pay us back?

The Danish philosopher and Christian writer Søren Kierkegaard once attended a very grand state service held in a huge cathedral in Copenhagen. All around him were the richest and most powerful people in the land: noblemen, captains of industry, the well read, the well bred and the well fed — the cream of society. Eventually the bishop began to address the congregation, preaching from the Magnificat:

And Mary said:
> 'My soul glorifies the Lord
>> and my spirit rejoices in God my Saviour,
> for he has been mindful
>> of the humble state of his servant.
> From now on all generations will call me blessed,
>> for the Mighty One has done great things for me—
>> holy is his name.
> His mercy extends to those who fear him,
>> from generation to generation.
> He has performed mighty deeds with his arm;
>> he has scattered those who are proud in their
>>> inmost thoughts.
> He has brought down rulers from their thrones
>> but has lifted up the humble.
> He has filled the hungry with good things
>> but has sent the rich away empty.'

(Luke 1:46–53)

As Kierkegaard listened, he looked around the cathedral at the people draped in ermine robes and dripping with gold and diamonds, and he cried—in fact he said that he cried because he couldn't understand why nobody was laughing.

Christ, of course, challenges us all to be generous with our money—financial greed is not necessarily a rich man's problem. Remember Jesus' parable of the widow's offering—or rather of her generosity with the few resources she had (Mark 12:41–44)? Each individual and each church is able to share financial resources at some level, and God loves a cheerful giver (2 Corinthians 9:7).

GENEROUS WITH OUR TIME

The problem is that generosity tends to be reduced down to questions of finance. A person is generous, we say, if he insists on picking up the bill at the end of a meal. However, while our attitudes to matters monetary are far from irrelevant, generosity can be expressed in many other ways. To view generosity in exclusively financial terms is misleading, excluding and minimizing. In fact, it lets us off the hook. If I'm financially rich, to part with my cash, even large sums, is not necessarily costly. But to give my time or share my expertise—now that might amount to true generosity.

In reading the story of Zacchaeus, it would be easy to overlook the significance of the fact that Jesus was surrounded by a throng of people. As any teacher or preacher knows, a large audience provides a great opportunity for a sermon. Jesus, however, chose not to spend his afternoon addressing the crowd but instead focused his attention and energy on one small, lonely and self-centred man in order to coax him out of his tree. He generously gave his valuable time to someone for whom nobody else did. It's not too great a stretch to consider that, had Jesus simply delivered a sermon within Zacchaeus's earshot, he would have remained hidden in his tree, listened with interest, perhaps even agreed with the points made, but returned to his work with his life largely unchanged.

Zacchaeus was not a nice man—by his own admission he had cheated and defrauded his own people and enjoyed a lavish and selfish lifestyle on the profits of his crime. Jesus never raises any of this with him, apparently not interested in condemning Zacchaeus but rather in building a relationship with him.

Important dynamics are at play in the transformation of Zacchaeus's life. First, Zacchaeus's own interest in finding out more about Jesus, which took him out of his way to get a closer look at him within the confines of his own safety zone. Second, Jesus' generosity to Zacchaeus. I venture to suggest that it wasn't primarily Jesus' words that changed Zacchaeus's life but that Jesus freely gave his time and attention to him. In a world aching from loneliness—a world where people, starved of friends and family, pay for advice because they desperately need attention—the most generous thing we can do is give our time.

I have a friend who is a doctor in a busy office. He tells me that he sees several of his patients often—they come in with any number of minor complaints—but their only real problem is that they are lonely. He asks his secretary to contact them if they miss an appointment because, as he puts it, 'When they don't come to see me, I realise they must be ill.'

BE GENEROUS WITH GRACE

A church can perhaps best display its generosity through its open-handedness with love. A generous church is a living, breathing demonstration that Leo Tolstoy was wrong when he famously claimed, 'The Christian churches and Christianity have nothing in common save in name: they are utterly hostile opposites. The churches are arrogance, violence, usurpation, rigidity, death; Christianity is humility, penitence, submissiveness, progress, life.'

A while ago I spoke at a large Christian conference. After I had delivered my message, one of the leaders marched up to me looking troubled. He asked if we could talk about some of the things I had said that night. In our conversation it emerged that he didn't like my attitude toward non-Christians. His belief was that, as an essential first step, the church's job is to ensure they understand that they are sinners. 'Let's keep the main thing the main thing,' he thundered. 'Sin is sin, and we have to name it as the nonnegotiable starting point in getting anyone to turn to Christ.' I disagree on several grounds, but mostly because I recognise that Jesus' way of approaching sinners does not cohere with this negative approach. Without doubt, Jesus did take a judgemental line, but he reserved it exclusively for one specific group—the religious leaders.

When a person knows she is lost, what she needs most are help and hope, not more hell. Inspire me; don't condemn me. I already know I'm lost. Instead of rubbing my lostness in my face, help me find a way out of it. Jesus offered a message of hope, of transformation, rather than one of condemnation and shame. Only one group allowed self-righteousness to blind them to their lostness or sense of need—and for them the blunt approach was the only option left.

American satirist H. L. Mencken writes, 'It is Hell, of course, that makes priests powerful, not Heaven, for after thousands of years of so-called civilization fear remains the one common denominator of mankind.' Over the centuries, too often the church has tried literally to scare the hell out of people. Indeed, it's how the infamous phrase originated. But fear is a poor motivation—generosity is stronger and ultimately far more powerful. In the words of theologian Walter Brueggemann, 'People are not changed by moral exhortation but by transformed imagination.'

Homer Simpson, that great caricature of a modern man, once exclaimed, 'I'm having the best day of my life, and I owe it all to not going to church.' How many people in our society does Homer speak for? It is a tragic truth that our churches are more known for what we are against than who we are for. Stop anyone in the street and ask them to cite some things that the church is opposed to, and they will come up with quite a list: sex, drugs, rock and roll, homosexuality, drinking, smoking, swearing, gambling, pornography, abortion, euthanasia and anyone who practices or promotes any of these things. Ask the same person to come up with some things that the church is for, and they will struggle. Have we become defined by our disdain?

Mother Teresa of Calcutta, who held firmly to the same views as many other Christians on issues such as abortion, euthanasia and sexuality, was not painted with a negative brush. She was better known for her generosity of spirit, her compassion, her willingness to serve and to sacrifice, her love and her grace than for anything else. It was not that her views on the issues above were not public, but simply that she demonstrated generosity — giving more, much more, than anyone could expect or bargain for. People understood that her stance on the issues was motivated by love. In other words, she was known for what she stood for — not just for what she stood against.

We must be known for our immovable commitment to the standards and values of Jesus — those of respect, faithfulness, love, grace, mercy, duty, justice, forgiveness, compassion and generosity — all born out of the genuine spirituality that results from a depth of relationship with God. The extent to which any local church is not primarily known for these qualities speaks of the challenge ahead of us.

The moment has come for the church to abandon, once and for all, a theology of judgement, a theology of in or out, sinner or saint, forgiven or not. We must more fully embrace a theology of inclusion, which is able to celebrate the goodness of creation without ignoring the great problem of sin. The time has come for the church to ensure that the main thing is the main thing.

Generous churches see the good in others and respond with a spirit of kindness and open-handedness rather than judgement. Generous churches see a person's potential before they see a person's problems. Generous churches acknowledge the issue of sin in each individual's life, but they do so within the context of recognising their own daily battle in this area. Generous churches do not look down on people; they look across at people. A generous church, to rephrase the words of the famous nineteenth-century Baptist preacher, C. H. Spurgeon, is a group of beggars telling other beggars where to find bread.

We are not some kind of universalist entity that says that everybody receives salvation whether or not they acknowledge Christ; instead we recognise the greatness and weakness in all people. None of us are perfect — all have fallen short. Generous mission starts with the simple but profound truth: 'God loves you whoever you are, whatever you've done, however scarred you are by sin. God loves you!' A generous church recognises that its tone and emphasis are as important as the core of its message.

Agostino d'Antonio, a sculptor of Florence, Italy, worked diligently but unsuccessfully on a large piece of marble for many months. Eventually he gave up; he simply could not do anything with the stone. Other sculptors worked with the piece of marble, but ultimately none could craft it into anything of beauty. The stone was discarded. It lay on a rubbish heap for forty years. That seemingly worthless piece of rock was to become one of the world's most famous pieces of renaissance art—Michelangelo's wonderful statue *David*. After its completion Michelangelo was often told how beautiful his work was. His standard reply was both simple and humble. All he had done, he said, was to reveal the beauty that was already hidden deep inside the marble. That is the task of a generous church—revealing the beauty that is already present in the lives of everyone we meet.

An intelligent church is a generous church.

YES, BUT HOW?

The hallmark of authentic generosity is giving what is of value to both the giver and the receiver. Real generosity is always costly—be it in terms of our time, our comments, our praise, our actions, our priorities, our opinions or our attitudes toward others. Generosity always comes with a price tag.

A generous church gives freely of its resources of money, time and space. When it engages in generous mission it weeps and mourns as well as laughs and celebrates. It gives people the benefit of the doubt rather than doubting their benefit. It recognises its own experience of the grace and mercy of God, and it shares from its own experience of God. It forgives and it doesn't condemn; it embraces and it doesn't exclude.

O   O   O

QUESTIONS

1. Work out ways that the congregation can play its part in meeting the spiritual, social and physical needs of your town and community. What are the big needs that are being left unmet in your area, and how can you as a Christian community do something to meet those needs in order to demonstrate God's generosity?

2. Think about ways in which you can use the space you have as a place of sanctuary and safety. Can you simply open your building more often? Can you have community gatherings where people can come and talk? Can you get out into the community to listen and talk to people more? Encourage your congregational members to consider how they can be generous at work or school. Encourage them to let people know that they are interested in them. Remind them to use their time a constructively — to offer a meal with folk who need support or volunteer to listen to someone who needs help.

3. Take a hard look at the church's finances. Which causes do you want to support with your benevolence fund? These causes might be community projects in your area or other sorts of work. Think about giving more money to these causes, and challenge your congregation to do the same. Set up a standing order for yourself each month. Consider setting up a charity account from which you can give, and teach your congregation how to do the same.

4. As a church, think about ways in which you can speak up on behalf of the excluded and the marginalized. Which campaigns can you get involved with as a community? Could you organise yourselves so that you can help those who have no voice to tell their story? Think

about campaigns for justice, debt cancellation, health or education; work out ways that you can get involved. Do certain causes in your town or community need your help or support? Encourage small groups to get involved.

5. Organise a special weekend during which you celebrate the achievements of your community. Perhaps you could award good citizen certificates, acknowledge the contribution of individuals in the community to its well-being, offer to publish a history of the area or plan a charity walk or a community picnic. On behalf of the church, write to the statutory bodies, thanking them for the good things they have done and asking them to come to a civic service. At that service commit to praying for them, and give them a signed copy of the Faithworks Charter (see the appendix: 'About Faithworks'). Organise other churches to get involved, and stand as one body for the good of your community.

CHAPTER 7

VULNERABLE
CHURCH

A n intelligent church is a vulnerable church. To be vulnerable means that you are capable of being hurt or damaged. 'When we were children, we used to think that when we were grown-up we would no longer be vulnerable,' says Madeleine L'Engle. 'But to grow up is to accept vulnerability....To be alive is to be vulnerable.'

JESUS WAS VULNERABLE

Jesus, the eternal Son of God through whom the cosmos was created (John 1:3), was born in a cave in the precivilized Middle East—utterly dependent on the care of those around him. The famous Christmas carol 'Away in a Manger' leaves us with an extremely romanticized and distorted impression of Jesus the infant. The line 'The little Lord Jesus, no crying he makes,' for instance, paints a picture of a serene baby who is somehow without the needs and responses that every other newborn faces. Had the little Lord Jesus stifled his cries when he needed to be fed, he may well have starved. Jesus was as vulnerable as any other baby; he needed every bit of the attention, nurture and protection that infanthood demands.

Before his birth Jesus became a single cell dividing into two, then four, then eight. God became an embryo in the womb of a young virgin. (Scholars speculate over Mary's exact age, some suggesting that she may have been as young as thirteen at the time of Jesus' birth.) To think that God placed his Son in the hands of an unmarried girl with no experience of motherhood is mind-stretching.

The vulnerability of Christ's birth becomes a pattern for his life. Whatever the strengths or weaknesses of Mel Gibson's film *The Passion of the Christ*, anyone who has seen it will be left in no doubt that God, in the person of Christ, made himself vulnerable. Though most of the film is focused on horrific scenes of Christ's torture and death, perhaps the subtlest and most compelling material concerns the account of his temptation in the garden of Gethsemane. I will never forget the picture of Jesus wrestling with his sense of anxiety, self-preservation and doubt, yet at the same time determined to fulfil his destiny. It is a portrait of a man stressed almost to the breaking point, who was in every sense vulnerable — physically, emotionally and spiritually. The Gospels present us with a real man locked in a human battle — a man whose eventual victory over his fears, and over the world's sin, does not lessen the pain of that long night.

The gospel writers' depiction of Jesus' day-to-day life reveals a man who lived with vulnerability and lack of security on all sides. He never owned a home. He did not marry. He had no material wealth. He was constantly misjudged. He spent the majority of his time with the sick, the unclean and the outcast. He embraced those with deadly diseases. He befriended his betrayer. He challenged the status quo. He violated the time-honoured religious taboos of his day. He became the enemy of the state.

NOT WEAKNESS

Vulnerability, though often mistaken for weakness or powerlessness, is not necessarily the same thing. While many of the world's most vulnerable people are powerless to change their situation, and weakness always leads to vulnerability, vulnerability itself is not synonymous with either.

The greatest example of this truth is, of course, Jesus. In him we discover someone who was vulnerable but whose vulnerability was a self-imposed choice rather than a condition that was thrust onto him by any external agent or force. The source of his vulnerability was his own sense of purpose and self-determination rather than any outside pressure he faced. He chose to be powerless; he was intentionally fragile. In Christ we encounter self-imposed vulnerability, the result of power purposely given up.

Jesus' vulnerability was the outcome of strength rather than weakness. His ability to make himself vulnerable is the direct outcome of his sense of self-understanding and self-esteem. He knew that he was God's Son, was secure within himself and, therefore, could not be demeaned by any task — even washing feet. The ability to make oneself vulnerable is always linked to security. In any relationship the more secure we are in ourselves, the more able we are to be vulnerable. Jesus himself commanded, 'Love your neighbour as yourself' (Matthew 22:39). The ability to love my neighbour is directly related to my self-esteem — the love I have for myself. When I don't love myself I will often come out fighting when otherwise I could have come out loving. As Elvis Presley's daughter, Lisa Marie, once said in an interview, 'I'm like a lion — I roar. If someone betrays me, I won't be a victim. I don't sulk, I get angry. I go immediately into retaliation. But it always comes from insecurity or pain.'

JESUS AS SERVANT

One of my favourite passages in the New Testament is John 13:1 – 17, the scene in which Jesus washes his disciples' feet.

It was just before the Passover Feast. Jesus knew that the time had come for him to leave this world and go to the Father. Having loved his own who were in the world, he now showed them the full extent of his love.

The evening meal was being served, and the devil had already prompted Judas Iscariot, son of Simon, to betray Jesus. Jesus knew that the Father had put all things under his power, and that he had come from God and was returning to God; so he got up from the meal, took off his outer clothing, and wrapped a towel around his waist. After that, he poured water into a basin and began to wash his disciples' feet, drying them with the towel that was wrapped around him.

He came to Simon Peter, who said to him, 'Lord, are you going to wash my feet?'

Jesus replied, 'You do not realise now what I am doing, but later you will understand.'

'No,' said Peter, 'you shall never wash my feet.'

Jesus answered, 'Unless I wash you, you have no part with me.'

'Then, Lord,' Simon Peter replied, 'not just my feet but my hands and my head as well!'

Jesus answered, 'A person who has had a bath needs only to wash his feet; his whole body is clean. And you are clean, though not every one of you.' For he knew who was going to betray him, and that was why he said not every one was clean.

When he had finished washing their feet, he put on his clothes and returned to his place. 'Do you understand what I have done for you?' he asked them. 'You call me "Teacher" and "Lord", and rightly so, for that is what I am. Now that I, your Lord and Teacher, have washed your feet, you also should wash one another's feet. I have set you an example that you should do as I have done for you. I tell you the truth, no servant is greater than his master, nor is a messenger greater than the one who sent him. Now that you know these things, you will be blessed if you do them.

Jesus, God incarnate, Creator of the world, knelt on a dusty floor and bathed twelve pairs of filthy feet—including one pair that belonged to the man he knew would soon betray him. Why did he do so? Indeed, how did he find the strength to do it? John's answers are clear. Jesus washed his disciples' feet to demonstrate his outrageous love for them. Jesus was able to wash his disciples' feet because he knew who he was and where he was going.

I often wonder why it is that of the two commands Jesus gave the disciples that day (the day before he was crucified)—to wash each other's feet and to remember him when they ate bread and drank wine—only one has been adopted as a church tradition. Why is it that we celebrate Communion, but we don't have foot-washing services? Perhaps the towel should be recognised as an international symbol of the Christian faith. Our God is the servant God, the foot-washing God, the vulnerable God. We are called to follow him.

JESUS AS LAMB

If the entire New Testament paints the same picture of Christ, the images contained in its last book, Revelation, press home the point. In Revelation 5, we read that 'the Lion of the tribe of Judah, the Root of David, has triumphed'—the only one who is worthy. But when John looks for the Lion of Judah in his vision, instead he sees a Lamb on the throne—and a slain, bloodstained Lamb at that.

Perhaps no other image in the entire New Testament is so vulnerable. It's as though John is saying to us, 'Every time you read Lion, think Lamb!' Here is the great secret at the heart of God: the magnificent, powerful, conquering Lion is at the same time the slain Lamb. This principle of vulnerability is built into the universe. From the beginning, the God who reveals himself as love has displayed his vulnerability. Since the beginning God has constantly been making himself vulnerable to humanity. He created the world that he might be in relationship with its citizens—but he has never chosen to force himself on us. He has constantly allowed people to reject him and his love. To love is always a painful experience and can even break your heart. As American poet Theodore Roethke put it, 'Love is not love until love's vulnerable.' God is vulnerable simply because he is love.

Isaiah 53 is one of the Old Testament's most moving, challenging and deeply humbling passages—one that the church has always seen as prophetically speaking of Christ. Written almost six hundred years before his birth, it is a commitment to powerlessness and self-giving that, at one and the same time, paints a picture of Jesus' vulnerability and challenges us about the very core of our Christian mission and motivation.

> Who has believed our message
>   and to whom has the arm of the LORD been
>   revealed?
> He grew up before him like a tender shoot,
>   and like a root out of dry ground.
> He had no beauty or majesty to attract us to him,
>   nothing in his appearance that we should desire
>   him.
> He was despised and rejected by men,
>   a man of sorrows, and familiar with suffering.
> Like one from whom men hide their faces
>   he was despised, and we esteemed him not.
> Surely he took up our infirmities
>   and carried our sorrows,
> yet we considered him stricken by God,
>   smitten by him, and afflicted.

But he was pierced for our transgressions,
    he was crushed for our iniquities;
the punishment that brought us peace was upon him,
    and by his wounds we are healed.
We all, like sheep, have gone astray,
    each of us has turned to his own way;
and the LORD has laid on him
    the iniquity of us all.
He was oppressed and afflicted,
    Yet he did not open his mouth;
he was led like a lamb to the slaughter,
    and as a sheep before her shearers is silent,
    so he did not open his mouth.

(verses 1–7)

BE LIKE JESUS

C. S. Lewis once observed that in a fierce storm only the reed that stands up against the wind without breaking feels its full force, not the one that is blown over. The entire act of incarnation, from beginning to end, whispers to us of a God who faces the full force of the storm as he becomes one of us—purposely choosing powerlessness, servanthood and vulnerability.

It is this kind of vulnerability that we are called to exhibit as we follow the way of Christ. For in serving selflessly we always make ourselves vulnerable. We give without any guaranteed return; we lay ourselves open to rejection and pain.

The challenge to us made in the hymn of Philippians 2 is as unambiguous as it is daunting:

Your attitude should be the same as that of Christ Jesus:
    Who, being in very nature God,
        did not consider equality with God something to be
            grasped,
    but made himself nothing,
        taking the very nature of a servant,
        being made in human likeness.

> And being found in appearance as a man,
>   he humbled himself
>   and became obedient to death—even death on a
>   cross!
>
> (verses 5–8)

The song concludes that Jesus emptied himself, that he made himself of no reputation, that he relinquished his rights, that he took upon himself the form of a servant, that he put others before himself. What does this mean for the church in its mission? How can our mission mirror the mission of God?

First Corinthians 13:4–8, like Philippians 2, was probably an early hymn. Although we have turned it into a wedding passage, it is clearly about the church's mission, its everyday relationships internally and externally—a set of relationships that reflect God himself.

> Love is patient, love is kind. It does not envy, it does not boast, it is not proud. It is not rude, it is not self-seeking, it is not easily angered, it keeps no record of wrongs. Love does not delight in evil but rejoices with the truth. It always protects, always trusts, always hopes, always perseveres.
>
> Love never fails.

Imagine these values, this ethos, shaping the mission of our lives and our churches. Mission that sought to be patient. Mission that sought to give people room. Mission that did not constantly compare itself to the things the church down the road was doing. Mission that did not exaggerate its effectiveness or indulge in the self-gratification of telling everyone about its successes but forgetting its mistakes and failures. Mission that gave people dignity but did not impose itself upon others. Mission that constantly sought to empower others to make choices and move forward rather than thinking it had to do it for them.

At the heart of a vulnerable church is the commitment to honour and respect people, irrespective of their background or position. It is the deep conviction that we as Christians should never use power or privilege to our own advantage. It is the ability to give ourselves away and to allow our own dreams and aspirations to die so that someone else might live. Vulnerable mission learns how to protect the weak instead of exploiting them and how to trust them rather than restrict them.

The Faithworks charter puts it plainly: 'We will provide an inclusive service to our community by serving and respecting all people regardless of their gender, marital status, race, ethnic origin, religion, age, sexual orientation or physical and mental capacity; by acknowledging the freedom of people of all faiths or none both to hold and to express their beliefs and convictions respectfully and freely; and by never imposing our Christian faith or belief on others.'

THE RESULT

First, when we make ourselves vulnerable, others are more likely to trust us. Oasis Trust, the charity that I set up in 1985, is building several secondary schools across England as part of a new government education initiative. As part of the planning process for one of them, a public meeting was held in the local civic centre for the Muslim community in which the school is to be built. Initially the meeting was quite hostile. Many of the local people could not understand why a Christian school was being built and were at first, understandably, uncomfortable with the whole idea.

One woman, looking angrily at me, aggressively shouted her question: 'Will you have a school uniform?' I hadn't really considered this point at the time and so answered her with a tentative yes. 'What colour will it be?' came her equally forceful response.

As I sat there, I realised something. I was a Christian, sitting on a stage, wearing a smart suit, telling these local people how we were going to transform education in their area with our thirty-million-pound budget and our shiny new school. These people, on the other hand, were poor; they didn't know me and had no reason to trust me. So rather than barking back a response to the woman's angry second question, I sat for a second before turning to her and saying gently, 'I don't know. What colour do you think it should be? Would you like to help to design it?'

In that instant the whole attitude of the meeting changed. In fact, at the end of the meeting, the local imam came up to me and told me that if we wanted to build other schools in Muslim areas around the country, he would come with us and be our envoy! Why did that meeting and the attitude of those people change? I believe that the small amount of vulnerability I demonstrated showed them that they could trust me.

Second, if we follow Jesus, we should frequently be guilty by association. If nobody ever accuses us, or at least suspects us, of compromise and moral failure because of the people we spend time with, then it's likely we are not spending enough time with the right people.

I once met a man called Dave who told me a fascinating story. He worked for a church project looking out for youngsters involved in gangs. He and a couple of others would go to meet gangs of young men as they hung around on the street corners and alleyways of South London. Most of the youngsters openly smoked cannabis, safe in the knowledge that the police would do little to stop them. Dave and his colleagues spent hours befriending them and began to have some success in building relationships with them.

One Sunday Dave was invited to visit a church in the neighbouring town to talk about his work and to recruit more volunteers for the scheme. However, before he even made it through the front door, an enormous elderly lady started shouting at him and then assaulted him with her umbrella. Eventually she was pulled off by another lady who was handing out hymnbooks.

Surprised by this less than warm welcome, Dave took several moments to work out what was going on. Still being held back and still spitting her accusations at him, the woman shouted, 'How dare you come in here? We don't want your drugs in here! I've seen you peddling poison to those boys! You should be ashamed of yourself. You're a child of Satan!'

Just one of the accusations that the religious leaders of his day levelled at Jesus and just one of the scenes we should expect in a vulnerable church. Intelligent Christians will always be vulnerable Christians, and vulnerability always hurts.

We model Christ's vulnerability when we, like him, identify with the pain and the struggles of our community. We model Christ's vulnerability when we, like him, become sufferers with people rather than commentators on their suffering. We model Christ's vulnerability when we stand with the excluded rather than apart from them. We model Christ's vulnerability when our reputations mean less to us than our compassion for others. We model Christ's vulnerability when we bear the wounds of our community, when we absorb and carry their fears in our hearts.

An intelligent church is a vulnerable church.

YES, BUT HOW?

The most profoundly incarnational acts are those where we, as individuals or churches, not only serve our communities but do so in projects we don't own and don't control—for in the end incarnation is fundamentally about giving up control. To sit with the minority group of the town council is incarnational. To serve on the Parent Teacher Association is incarnational. To run the summer dance at the local school is incarnational. To put our influence, energy, time, money and enthusiasm into helping to build a much-needed community nursery school or to join the campaign for a new road crossing—these things are incarnational. Why? Because each demands that we give without building our own empires. Because each is costly. Because each is a twenty-first-century equivalent of washing feet.

When I first became a minister, as part of my ordination ceremony, I was asked to promise to serve God's people—to pastor, teach, pray for, encourage, equip and support them. But I was struck that these promises related only to the church. In every local church-based interview I have had since, I have always been asked the same kind of questions: 'Why do you feel called to this church?' I have never been asked anything like 'Why do you feel called to serve this local community? What do you know about this area? What is your vision for it?'

We will become truly incarnational, and echo the mission of Christ, only when we have the courage to lift our eyes from the needs of our churches and congregations to serve our whole communities—giving up control and working as part of them rather than apart from them. This will be costly. It will hurt, and it will make us vulnerable—and therefore more effective.

○   ○   ○

QUESTIONS

1. How can you as a church use the influence you have been given by God to serve your community? Explore ways in which you can use your influence for those who have no power. This might include speaking up for those of other faiths who are being persecuted, identifying yourselves with immigrants or asylum seekers or working for those in poor-quality housing.

2. Be bold enough to explore ways in which you have used power badly. Have you exploited your congrega-

tion or one another? Apologize for that and organise a time of repentance and reconciliation for those in the congregation. Perhaps the church leadership could model vulnerability by serving Communion and by washing the feet of those who come. Be careful not to become tokenistic, but at the same time be bold enough to embrace the symbolism of what you are doing.

3. Identify key champions in the community or the congregation and work out ways of supporting them and investing in them for the future. Be bold enough to take a risk.

4. Allow time in your meetings for vulnerability and transparency. Begin to explore ways in which all of your small groups can build these traits into their DNA. Encourage an atmosphere of mutual accountability by modelling it.

5. Start exploring ways of giving yourselves away. This might mean doing things differently, letting others have their say while you remain silent or getting behind projects and ideas that are already happening rather than having to be at the centre all the time. Seek to honour others and to praise the work of other Christians and other churches.

CHAPTER 8

POLITICAL
CHURCH

A n intelligent church is a political church. I remember as a boy my father complaining to my mother, over Sunday lunch, that 'the problem with that new minister of ours is that he keeps trying to drag politics into the pulpit. The pulpit is not the place for politics.' So it was that I grew up with the old adage that politics and religion don't mix.

I have subsequently come to understand that, far from being incompatible, politics and Christianity are, in reality, inseparable. What don't mix are Christianity and social apathy. The English word *politics* is derived from the Greek *polis*, which literally means 'city'—hence politics is simply the affairs of the city. Desmond Tutu said, 'If we are to say that religion cannot be concerned with politics, then we are really saying that there is a substantial part of human life in which God's will does not run.' The veteran Archbishop and anti-apartheid campaigner concluded by asking a telling question: 'If it is not God's, then whose is it?'

JESUS WAS A POLITICIAN

Bishop N. T. Wright, the author and theologian, has argued effectively that whatever Jesus wasn't, he was a politician. Jesus would have been recognised first and foremost as a politician by his contemporaries, not as the simple preacher we have often portrayed him as. Why? Because Jesus had an agenda not just for individuals but for the way in which the whole of society operated. His message was not just of personal transformation but of societal renewal.

Jesus stood up in the synagogue in Nazareth at the beginning of the three years he would spend in the public eye in order to deliver his famous manifesto:

> The Spirit of the Lord is on me,
>   because he has anointed me
>   to preach good news to the poor.
> He has sent me to proclaim freedom for the prisoners
>   and recovery of sight for the blind,
> to release the oppressed,
>   to proclaim the year of the Lord's favour.
>
> (Luke 4:18–19)

It would have been impossible to make a more powerful or provocative political statement. First, Jesus was deliberately reading from a passage of the Old Testament that the Jewish people regarded as being messianic, that is, referring to the role that their long-awaited liberator would play. Second, he provocatively chose to add the sentence, 'Today this scripture is fulfilled in your hearing' (Luke 4:21).

It is only as you grasp the context of the culture in which Jesus lived and worked that you can begin to understand the full extent of the political nature of his message. Israel was a proud but troubled nation that had long lived with the ignominy and tragedy of occupation by a foreign power. The book of Genesis records the promise God made to Abram (the founding father of the Jewish people) that his descendents would inherit a piece of land they would forever call their own. This same wonderful promise was repeated centuries later to Moses, and eventually, shortly after his death, the Israelites finally took possession of Canaan, a land 'flowing with milk and honey'. However, if the Promised Land was not easily gained (it took a daring escape from slavery in Egypt, a forty-year sojourn in a desert, many bloody battles and huge amounts of faith), this all paled into insignificance when compared to the struggle to maintain it.

In Jesus' time, though the people of Israel still believed the land was theirs—the divine fulfilment of aged promises—they lived each day with the painful memories of invasion, conquer and exile and of the broken line of the royal family of David. But more than that, they lived with the reality of the continuing, present-day oppression of the Roman army.

The Romans were just the latest in a long line of hated occupying forces Israel had endured over the centuries—enemies whom every true Israelite could not wait to see ousted. So it was that the Jews prayed for, longed for and actively anticipated the coming of the messiah (the anointed one)—the prophesied political leader who would free them and return the Promised Land to its rightful heirs. In the words of Martin Luther King Jr, a freedom fighter from an age yet to be, the Jews longed for the day when they would be able to join hands and sing, 'Free at last! Free at last! Thank God Almighty, we are free at last.'

From time to time Israel's recent history had been punctuated by the emergence of another would-be messiah, but always with the eventual result of failure in a merciless bloodbath—crushing the hopes of the people once again. Indeed, until Jesus, all messianic candidates had proven to be pretenders to the throne simply because they failed to achieve the one goal by which a successful messiah was measured: freedom.

In our twenty-first-century thinking, the title *Messiah* confers divinity; it is a word synonymous with God. For us the two roles are intrinsically linked, but that wasn't the case in the minds of the Jews. Rather than conferring divinity, *messiah* indicated political prowess for the people of Israel. The messiah was a political deliverer—the chosen agent of God, but not himself divine. Though Jesus' claim to divinity was consistent, clear and unambiguous, even he in applying the title messiah to himself was not claiming to be divine. He was instead declaring to Israel that he was God's agent for change. Jesus, then, must have had a political message that resonated with those who heard his teaching—why else would they declare him to be the true Messiah, the fulfilment of their years of longing? The gospel writer John tells us that 'Andrew, Simon Peter's brother, was one of the two who heard what John had said and who had followed Jesus. The first thing Andrew did was to find his brother Simon and tell him, "We have found the Messiah" (that is, the Christ). And he brought him to Jesus' (John 1:40–42).

THE MESSAGE OF THE MESSIAH

Standing at a distance of two millennia, and looking through endless cultural filters that have blurred the clarity of our image, we tend to forget just how radical Jesus' message and politics were. But for his original audience, his reading of Isaiah 61, along with his subsequent comment, was nothing short of a public declaration of political intent. His words were so inflammatory, as we learn in Luke 4:29, that the people in the synagogue drove him out of the town and took him to the brow of the hill on which the town was built in order to throw him down the cliff. A strong reaction to a Bible reading and sermon by anyone's standards.

Why such a strong reaction? Not because of his initial claim to be the Messiah—that may have surprised them, and it certainly intrigued them, but it didn't anger them to the point of attempted murder. No, what really incensed them was that, using two illustrations from the life of Elijah, Jesus began to talk of his task and God's intention to bring salvation beyond Israel (Luke 4:24–27).

Everyone has heard a handful of sermons on the theme of how radically different Jesus was from the popular first-century Jewish expectation of the long-awaited Messiah: the Jewish people looked for a powerful political leader; instead Jesus arrived as the humble servant-king. Jesus was a very different kind of Messiah — far from the swash-buckling, conquering hero the Jews were expecting and hoping for.

What marked him as different, though, was not that he was political — every would-be messiah was exactly that. For example, as Howard Marshall explains, 'When Simon bar Koseba led the Jews in their second war of independence against Rome (AD 132 – 135) he was hailed by a leading rabbi as the King, the Messiah. What set Jesus apart was the radical nature of his politics.' As far as Jesus' contemporaries were concerned, God's liberation was a military liberation and a Jewish liberation. The messiah was a Jewish messiah — nothing more, nothing less. End of story.

Jesus, however, was claiming not only to be the Messiah but also to be a very different kind of Messiah. He smashed their expectations. 'I'm the Messiah. I'll set you free, but not in the way you are expecting.' Jesus had come to bring liberation, but a different kind of liberation and not just for respectable Jews. Jesus had come preaching regime change — but the wrong kind of regime change, as far as they were concerned.

Jesus' central political theme becomes even clearer in his Sermon on the Mount, in which he announced that the poor and the excluded count in the kingdom of God. Even the location he chose was significant. His sermon was not delivered in the temple or a synagogue, nor was it given to an audience of scholars and religious leaders; instead it was preached on a hillside to a collection of spiritual zeros and social misfits — the very people who had been failed so desperately by Israel's dysfunctional model of community. Though Israel's religious leaders had treated these people as outcasts, Jesus told them that in his version of the long-awaited kingdom of God, they were to be included, not excluded; to be players, not spectators. Not only was he offering the outcasts, the forgotten, the oppressed and the overlooked of his society the opportunity of inclusion, but also, and more controversially, he was preaching a complete reversal of the status quo—a reorganisation of society.

> Blessed are the poor in spirit,
>   for theirs is the kingdom of heaven....
> You are the light of the world. A city on a hill cannot be hidden. Neither do people light a lamp and put it under a bowl. Instead they put it on its stand, and it gives light to everyone in the house. In the same way, let your light shine before men, that they may see your good deeds and praise your Father in heaven.
>
> (Matthew 5:3, 14–16)

It was the misfits who would lead the revolution.

Jesus taught that the kingdom of heaven is located in time and space and begins in the here and now. Though many twenty-first-century Christians—who have come to regard God's kingdom as being solely about an otherworldly, pie in the sky when you die, life beyond death experience—may be surprised, his message was no shock to his Jewish audience who were actively anticipating the day of the Lord—the day of liberation in their lifetime.

However, the second aspect of the vision of the kingdom of God that Jesus proclaimed did shock his original audience: life would be turned upside down; many who had been elevated would discover themselves to be least important, and those who had been overlooked would be prominent. 'Many who are first will be last, and many who are last will be first' (Matthew 19:30).

And perhaps the church in the West, twenty-one centuries later, has still not fully absorbed the explosive impact of these words.

HOW JESUS GOT INVOLVED

Although Jesus said very little directly to the Roman authorities, his words and actions sent them the same clear political
message that he gave to his followers—God was on the side
of the oppressed, the excluded and the marginalized. Take, for
instance, just one tiny example: Jesus' teaching about going
the extra mile that he gives as part of the Sermon on the
Mount. 'If someone forces you to go one mile, go with him
two miles' (Matthew 5:41). This curious little verse is actually
deeply subversive. It refers to the fact that under military law,
any Roman soldier could require a Jew to carry his kit bag
for a distance of up to a mile. At any time, therefore, a soldier
could demand that a Jew became his temporary slave—there
were no exemptions.

The Romans prided themselves on their discipline and firm
commitment to the rule of the law. For a soldier to force a
Jew to bear his load for more than the regulation mile was
illegal—and any breach of the law was dealt with severely. It is
only as we understand this that we begin to grasp the subversive
nature of Jesus' words. Far from instructing them to act like
doormats by meekly submitting to oppression, Jesus was calling
them to deal a blow to the system through a deliberate act of
rebellion via generous civil disobedience. He was deliberately
setting out a strategy that would underline the dignity, spirit and
freedom of those who were oppressed—and at the same time
put their oppressors in a spin. The crowd would have laughed
as Jesus talked. It was a wonderful thought—a soldier, fearful of
punishment, begging his slave to put down his load and leave
him alone. The tables were turned. It was direct action, it was
political, it was deeply subversive—but it was nonviolent.

The group that Jesus far more frequently confronted were
the Pharisees and the rest of the Jewish hierarchy. In the common twenty-first-century perception, the Pharisees are often

caricatured as a sinister group of wholly evil men—the religious leaders who plotted to kill Jesus. While it is true that they were often at loggerheads with Jesus and were deeply implicated in the orchestration of his political execution, their motivation (as misguided as it was) was a passionate concern for the preservation of Judaism and the worship of Yahweh in the face of the corrupting religions of Rome and Greece. The Pharisees were neither wholly evil nor solely concerned with religious matters.

The precise origins of the Pharisees are unclear. Indeed, were we reliant on the Bible for an accurate history of the period, we would have to conclude that they simply appeared out of thin air. Fortunately, though, we have many additional sources of historical information—most notably a famed Jewish historian named Josephus, who himself claimed to be a Pharisee. The first mention that Josephus gives to the existence of the sect is around 100 BC.

The Pharisees were dedicated to observing the Law as laid out in the Torah (the first five books of the Old Testament), but they felt it needed interpretation in order for it to relate to modern life. It is important to understand that even this additional interpretation was driven by their deep reverence for God and a desire to honour him. In fact, they came to believe that if they could get all of Israel to keep the whole of the law for a single day, God's kingdom would come—the Romans' reign would end and Israel would be free to fulfil its original calling. This desire led them to develop an Oral Law (or oral Torah) as a commentary on, or guide to, the written Torah.

Over time they reached the belief that they, and only they, held the keys to the Torah's authentic interpretation. They held a monopoly on the truth. Their word was literally law. They assumed they had a God-given authority to decide what was acceptable and what wasn't. In their efforts to get everyone to live within the bounds of the Law as they understood it, they laid out precise rules governing every aspect and element of life for the Jews. For example, the written Law states that the Sabbath should be kept holy; it should not be a time for work (Exodus 16:23; 20:8; 35:2 and others). In their oral interpretation of this originally grace- and freedom-filled command, the Pharisees set out to define exactly what work was and wasn't. They decreed that any physically straining activity, such as carrying firewood, was not permissible whatever the circumstances (a ridiculous conclusion that totally missed the intention of the concept of Sabbath).

They didn't stop there. By the time of Jesus their interpretation of the Law had reached such levels of micromanagement that they had ruled that if someone got a splinter in their finger on the Sabbath, they couldn't do the work of removing it and therefore would have to sit out the rest of the day—because to carry on walking around with the splinter was classed as carrying wood, which was also work and therefore another breach of the Law.

Take another example: The Pharisees, by the same contorted logic, had decided that spitting on the ground on the Sabbath constituted making a brick and was, therefore, equated with labour—hence their outrage when Jesus spat on the ground and placed the mud on the eyes of the blind man. All the Pharisees could see was that Jesus was breaking the rules upon which contemporary, respectable Jewish society was established.

Why did Jesus spit on the ground to heal the blind man? It's a question that every Sunday school child has asked but one that is rarely answered. Did he do it to heal the blind man (also a sin on the Sabbath)? No. We know that Jesus healed many people without spitting. His saliva wasn't some sort of magic medicine. Instead, he did it to challenge the prevailing social order and religious values of Israel. It was a political act. 'First, I'm going to make a brick on the Sabbath. Second, I'm going to heal this man on the Sabbath. Which do you want to take most offence at?'

Considering the priests and Pharisees of Jesus' day simply as religious leaders is widely missing the mark. Israel had a unique sociopolitical structure that made it unlike any society with which we might attempt to compare her today; it was a theocracy. Yahweh was regarded as the supreme ruler of Israel; other institutions of governance (such as judges and kings) existed only to serve him. In such a society, the power and the position of religious leaders were vast. In Israel, unlike in our secularized societies, religion was concerned with and integrated into all aspects of life. The influence of the religious leaders pervaded everywhere. They were the community leaders, the town council members, the statesmen, the diplomats, the teachers. Since God is concerned with all areas of life, no area was outside the interests of religious leadership.

THE POLITICAL CHURCH

In Western democracies, *politics* has become a dirty word. The church has a vital role to play in challenging this perception. Local congregations do not have the option of choosing to engage in the needs of their communities; they have a responsibility to do so. Far from being incompatible, Christianity and politics are inseparable. Wherever real needs exist, the church has a God-given — Christ-inspired — mandate to be engaged. Asylum, poverty, people trafficking, housing, education, employment, healthcare, youth issues, crime, marriage, community development, the environment, regeneration, international relief, trade justice, globalization, human rights, taxation, addiction, discrimination, care of the elderly, foreign policy, mental health and national and local council spending priorities are just a few areas where real needs exist.

The story is told of a man who sat and waited by a fast-flowing river. Every so often a person was washed over the rapids, and the man sprang into action. He tied one end of a rope to a tree and the other around his waist and jumped into the water. A strong swimmer, he sped toward the drowning

soul and, nine times out of ten, managed to pull the person
to shore. The man saved a great many lives—but how many
more would be spared if, one day, instead of sitting and waiting
for another floundering person to be swept over the rocks, he
walked upstream and fixed the wobbly bridge that caused them
to fall into the river?

It's right and proper that our churches should operate projects and programmes that help the homeless, the hopeless and
the socially excluded—but ultimately these are nothing more
than sticking-plaster solutions. How much more effective
would we be if we spent more of our energies campaigning for
these problems and evils, often upheld through vested interest,
to be eradicated at the source?

A political church is a church with a mission to meet the
needs of people as individuals as well as whole communities. A
political church is a church with a mission to meet social and
economic needs as well as those that are spiritual and emotional. A political church is a church with a mission to help
people find answers to the problems and challenges they face,
but also to help them deal with the reasons those problems
and challenges exist in the first place. A political church is a
church that understands that its mission must move beyond
social action to the quest for social justice. A political church
not only helps pull people out of the river; it works to find
ways of stopping them from falling into the river in the first
place. As American author Jim Wallis said, 'We need a politics
that offers us something we haven't had in a long time: a vision
of transformation.'

PROPHETIC ROLE

The political church must be careful to avoid becoming a
mouthpiece for one political view or party. The church must be
politically engaged with the affairs of society but must remain
an independent voice—refusing to be annexed to, or forced

into the pocket of, any one political party, system or view. Our very independence gives us our unique prophetic role in the political process, and we give it up at our peril.

The church's role is similar to that of the Old Testament prophets—to be the voice of the concerned outsider. The prophets were never in bed with the establishment. They did not aim, nor did they need, to please the rulers. Rather, their task was to ensure that God's agenda was not neglected in the day-to-day running of Israel. John the Baptist, in the tradition of the great Old Testament prophets (Isaiah, Daniel, Elijah, Samuel), had access to the king, but he was never in the king's pocket. A healthy tension should always exist between church and state as it existed between prophet and king. The church has a responsibility to be a critical friend that respects but also challenges government. In the words of the prophet Amos—emblazoned across the Martin Luther King Jr memorial in Washington—we are to strive to see 'justice roll on like a river, righteousness like a never-failing stream' (Amos 5:24).

If we want to be a recognised voice in society, we have to seriously up our engagement with the issues. Charles Spurgeon said, 'The Christian preacher carries a Bible in one hand and a newspaper in the other—and reads them both!' We have to grapple with the issues of our culture as well as the word of God—the two making sense of each other. J. C. Ryle writes:

> When St. Paul says, 'Come out and be separate,' he did not mean that Christians ought to take no interest in anything on earth except religion. To neglect science, art, literature and politics—to read nothing which is not directly spiritual—to know nothing about what is going on among mankind, and never to look at a newspaper—to care nothing about the government of one's own country, and to be utterly indifferent to the persons who guide its counsels and make its laws—all of this may seem very right and proper in the eyes of some people. But I take leave to think that it is an idle, selfish neglect of duty.

The task of every intelligent church is to be involved in the affairs of its community and society at large.

An intelligent church is a political church.

YES, BUT HOW?

To paint a picture of Jesus as apolitical misunderstands not only him but also the impact that he made and the scope of the challenge he brought to the Jewish hierarchy. Furthermore, it further strengthens the false division of sacred and secular on which our society is built but of which the Bible knows very little. Jesus' mission touched every part of life. It offered God's shalom, or well-being, for every area of life — spiritual, physical, emotional, social and, by extension, political. The church's mission is just as rounded and political. A gospel that offers anything less is no gospel at all.

○   ○   ○

QUESTIONS

1. A good place to start is by working out what issues your church community is passionate about. Some will be passionate about one topic, while others will be passionate about something else. The most likely situation will be that you have a number of different issues that will be important to your congregation. Once you know what these are, you need to work out strategically how you can best respond to each of them. It's here that you will need to be committed to teamwork, because no one person will ever do it all.

2. Whatever the issues, make a list of them so that you don't try to do everything at once. Then find champions for each cause and get them talking about how they could move things forward. If you recognise that

someone in the congregation is passionate about an issue, talk to him about what he does to make a difference. It might be he ends up becoming a link to other organisations that work in that area.

3. Keep your eyes and ears open so that you can pick up what national advocacy campaigns are taking place. Ones to look out for will be debt cancellation, trade justice, human trafficking and poverty. All of these have great organisations that work to raise the issue and provide solutions. Encourage your church to link into the campaigns that are most relevant to you.

4. In the run-up to local elections or general elections, use your buildings and resources as a tool to highlight the issues that are important and help candidates to address them. Many organisations can help you to get involved in the political process, and they will be the best place to start. You can do that through holding community meetings, organising interviews with candidates and trying to get onto panels that address the key issues. Be careful not to appear to be a church that supports only one party. See your role as a prophetic one in which the church challenges political priorities. You can celebrate what is good, and you can speak out for what could be better.

5. Keep the prayer life of the church alive and topical. Instead of praying just for those inside the church, make a regular commitment to highlight the issues the community is facing and pray about them. Give public time to praying through some of the issues in your community regularly, and consider writing a community prayer that highlights the issues the community is facing.

6. Broaden the agenda of your political engagement. Make people aware of the issues they should think through.

Traditionally, the church has become political over the big moral arguments of abortion, euthanasia and homosexuality. While you may well have strong views on all of these, also work for justice on such issues as poverty, education, crime and housing. If you are able to, make an appointment to see your mayor or your congressperson and talk through the concerns and ideas that you have. If you feel closely aligned with one party, then join it. Consider supporting the candidate or even standing yourself at some point.

CHAPTER 9

DIVERSE
CHURCH

An intelligent church is a diverse church. 'Diversity makes for a rich tapestry,' says Maya Angelou. The greater the number of threads in the tapestry of any local church, the more attractive and effective it becomes.

An intelligent church celebrates diversity—it values the unique contributions and ideas that every member of the community of faith brings because of who they are and what they do. For some churches this is unthinkable. For others it is welcome. For all it is challenging. A diverse mission strategy is built upon the premise that all who are part of the community of faith are already engaged in mission—as teachers, builders, college students, doctors, lawyers, factory workers, health workers, shopkeepers, artists. It recognises that God gave us our gender, our skills, our abilities and our interests for a reason, and that the church exists to train, equip and release all within the body for the work of building God's kingdom. It means that the focus of our teaching, discipleship, preaching and training changes. It means our understanding of worship, holiness and devotion is transformed. It means nothing short of a revolution in our thinking and action.

GOD CREATED DIVERSITY

God's creation is so kaleidoscopic in its diversity as to be almost beyond comprehension. The number of different kinds of insects alone defies belief—we have identified well over a million, and biologists inform us that their best guess is that countless species are yet to be discovered. For instance, the over three hundred thousand known varieties of beetles led biologist J. B. S. Haldane to consider that 'God has an inordinate fondness for beetles.' Why, one must ask, did God make creation so diverse? One can assume only that the wealth of life on earth is due to God's extravagance. He created the squirrel not because of any real need for squirrels but because he liked the idea of squirrels. Looking upon the natural world, it is easy to sense God's sheer joy in creation—you can imagine the delight he felt when he came up with the ridiculous idea of giraffes.

A friend of mine has a young daughter named Helena who used to have a favourite television show. The impact of this programme on Helena was always the same; whatever her mood she was instantly mesmerized. My friend said that she would happily watch the same episode over and over again. And through it she learnt her first word: *gen*. *Gen* is toddlerish for *again*. And Helena was more than happy wandering round the house saying 'gen' to anything and everything. When she was fed her tea—'gen.' When she was tickled—'gen.' When she was read a story—'gen.' The author G. K. Chesterton paints a wonderful picture of God being so carried away with the beauty of his creation that he wanders around it repeating one word: 'gen.' Gen to the sunrise every new morning, gen to snow drops every spring, gen to the birth of every new baby, gen to the snows of winter each year, gen to every reddened sky at sunset, gen to every starry night. 'It may be that God makes every daisy separately but has never got tired of making them,' Chesterton remarks. 'It may be that he has the eternal appetite of infancy; for we have sinned and grown old, and our Father is younger than we.'

Alphonso the Wise, the king of Castile and Leon in the thirteenth century, once remarked, 'Had I been present at the creation, I would have given some useful hints for the better ordering of the universe.' It's an interesting notion—what would the world have been like if one of us had been involved in its creation. We would have doubtless decided that night and day was a good idea, but would we have arranged the transition from one to the other so beautifully? God offered extravagant generosity to creation and its ongoing nature that even Alphonso might have struggled to replicate.

GOD IS DIVERSE

The diversity of creation is simply a reflection of who God is. God is diverse. God is triune—three in one. It is often said that the most profound theological statement in the whole Bible is that 'God is love' (1 John 4:8). The truth is that were God a single person, if he were one rather than three and one, we could not know him as love. As theologian Stanley Grenz put it, 'Self-love cannot be true charity, supreme love requires another, equal to the lover, who is the recipient of that love, and because supreme love is received as well as given, it must be a shared love, in which each person loves and is loved by the other.'

If God were just one and not three, then he could not be intrinsically love because until he created the world he would have had nothing to love. Michael Lloyd explains this clearly in his book *Café Theology*: 'For "most" of eternity he would not have been involved in a loving relationship. He would be dependent upon the world to provide an object for his love.' It is only because the Father, Son and Spirit respond to each other in constantly loving relationships that we can say that the very nature of God is love.

The doctrine of the Trinity tells us that God is a community. God is in constant internal relationship. Three persons — Father, Son and Spirit — one in substance (or essence), are actually defined by their relationships with one another and their distinctiveness from one another. The Father is in relationship with the Son by the Spirit and cannot be the Father other than through this relationship, since without the Son he would not be the Father. The profound truth is that God is a diverse but united society within himself. Colin Gunton explains:

> God is a fellowship of persons whose orientation is entirely to the other. The notion of there being three persons in God is problematic for us, because we think that person means individual in the modern sense of one whose being is defined over against, even in opposition to, other individuals.... The Trinitarian notion of person does incorporate one aspect of the notion of individuality, because it holds that each person is unique and irreplaceable. The Father is not the Son, the Son is not the Spirit, and all three of them are essential to God's being as God. On the other hand, these three are, while distinct from one another, not in competition, as in modern individualism, but entirely for and from one another. There is accordingly an orientation to the other within the eternal structure of God's being.

CHURCH IMITATES

God, by his very nature, is diverse — but at the same time lives in absolute unity without competition or individualism. The goal of every intelligent church is to imitate or reflect this unity in diversity.

Paul writes to the Corinthians:

> The body is a unit, though it is made up of many parts; and though all its parts are many, they form one body. So it is with Christ. For we were all baptized by one Spirit into one body — whether Jews or Greeks, slave or free — and we were all given the one Spirit to drink....

The eye cannot say to the hand, 'I don't need you!' And the
head cannot say to the feet, 'I don't need you!' On the contrary,
those parts of the body that seem to be weaker are indispens-
able, and the parts that we think are less honourable we treat
with special honour....

Now you are the body of Christ, and each one of you is a
part of it.
                          (1 Corinthians 12:12–13, 21–23, 27)

The Trinity is characterized by mutuality and service rather
than domination, hierarchy and lordship. This, claims theologian Jurgen Moltmann, should also serve as the critical principle for the church in its mission to transform the world. In
the words of Pope Benedict XVI, this should be the 'communal
shape of the Christian faith'.

COMMUNITY IMPROVES INDIVIDUALS

Through the fall, human personhood is perverted. Though
we are still in the image of God, our current state means this
is true only in a disrupted fashion and as an unfulfilled tendency. We have become individualistic and have learnt to affirm
ourselves over against, and at the expense of, one another and
God. Still, the church constitutes the body of Christ—with a
mission to bring deindividualization and, as a result, bring true
and diverse community.

All this is an essential part of what Jesus meant when he
taught that he had come to bring abundant life or life to the
full, to lead us toward being fully human. So it is that a diverse
church provides the best kind of community for personal
development. The opportunity to work with other people in a
supportive framework is one that allows individuals to develop
and realise potential that otherwise may have been forever
overlooked, as well as to be held accountable—which is the
best solution for the removal of all those rough edges.

Besides being a writer, John Donne was dean of Saint Paul's
Cathedral in London. He held a view of society as rooted in

the life of the Trinity, which he once described as a 'holy and whole college'. It was just before his death in 1631 that he penned his famous words:

> All mankind is of one author, and is one volume; when one man dies, one chapter is not torn out of the book, but translated into a better language; and every chapter must be so translated.... As therefore the bell that rings to a sermon, calls not upon the preacher only, but upon the congregation to come: so this bell calls us all: but how much more me, who am brought so near the door by this sickness.... No man is an island, entire of itself; every man is a piece of the continent, a part of the main ... any man's death diminishes me, because I am involved in mankind; and therefore never send to know for whom the bell tolls; it tolls for thee.

Being part of a community brings a sense of identity, security and accountability—vital not only to human development and fulfilment but also to survival. We are not independent; we are interdependent. The diversity of community makes economical, creative, psychological, strategic and social sense primarily because that's the way God made us and intends us to work. No one is an island. We need each other in order to experience true human life, and we need each other in order to accomplish anything of lasting worth during that life.

INDIVIDUALS IMPROVE COMMUNITIES

It is ludicrous to suggest that all people are the same—that each racial, ethnic or interest group bears the same characteristics and that no difference exists between the genders. Diversity is about acknowledging not only that we are all different but also that, when we embrace those differences, together we make a stronger, healthier community.

Our differences are not a weakness. Our diversity is our great strength. Just as a body entirely composed of hands would be useless, a church that contains only one type of person would accomplish little. Occupational psychologists Michael Pearn and Rajvinder Kandola wrote: 'Diversity is founded on the premise that harnessing the difference will create a productive environment in which everyone feels valued, where their talents are being fully utilized and in which organisational goals are met.'

The manufacturers of computers are always keen to boast about the number of colours their machines can display. The first computer I ever used showed everything in two shades — green and black. This soon developed into eight colours, then sixteen, then thirty-two — and today millions. The detection of subtle differences improves the quality of the picture.

Diversity is essential to every intelligent church. Any leader surrounded by a skilled and diverse team will be more effective. 'As iron sharpens iron, so one man sharpens another' claims Proverbs 27:17. It's a tried and tested way of getting things done. It's the logical way to achieve any task and at the same time give people the opportunity to develop their gifts and skills and be involved. A good (and therefore diverse) church reacts quicker, moves faster, thinks smarter and can actually achieve far more than the sum of the individuals who make it up.

Although we usually assume that our tactic is the best (that's why we're doing it that way), we have to admit that goals can be achieved in various manners. Diversity generates stronger and more creative ideas and so produces more imaginative solutions to problems than are likely to result from the best efforts of a single mind. The result of being surrounded by others who will always agree with you is mediocrity. Personal growth and community creativity are born out of the tension of differing opinions, approaches and insights. Any healthy team is bound to feel the tension sometimes. If there's never any edginess to our work, perhaps we've simply gone to sleep on the task.

Here is a truth that has taken me half a lifetime to acknowledge: I am not balanced. I never will be. Indeed, I am incapable of achieving true balance. My personality—the way in which God has wired me—means that I see things in a particular way, through a specific set of lenses. My goal is no longer to be the balanced all-rounder that I thought I should be. The balance exists in the body, not in the individual members. I need others who see life through different lenses to work with me as a corrective. They need me as much as I need them, for they are not balanced either. Only together can we find what eludes us as individuals. Each hand must be wholeheartedly a hand—to attempt to also do the job of a foot would be foolish. I must bring what I bring without compromise. In the context of a diverse church, my contribution will be honed, shaped and balanced by others. Thus I, and we, will be held accountable, will flourish and grow.

Though it can sometimes be threatening to be with people who do not think, act and behave like us, that very diversity brings us depth, breadth and vibrancy. Conversely, sameness always leads to blandness and mediocrity. The quest for uniformity is like pureeing mixed fruit in a blender—all of the constituent parts are present, but it becomes impossible to discern any individual colours, forms, textures or flavours. What you end up with is all boringly the same.

Diversity recognises that we are not all the same; we are unique and equally valuable. Diversity is like a fruit salad rather than a fruit puree. In a fruit salad each individual piece of fruit retains its unique characteristics while, at exactly the same time, the different fruits mix and enhance one another. The sharpness of pineapple is offset by the sweetness of pear, the smoothness of banana by the citrus bite of orange.

THE ORIGINAL PURPOSE OF CHURCH

In the New Testament, the word *church* literally means a 'called out' people or society. Originally the term was also used to describe other associations of people joined together by a common purpose. Its very name indicates that the church was never intended to function as a loose collection of individualistic, independent players. It was always supposed to be interdependent, recognising and benefiting from each other's gifts, strengths and abilities.

Paul, in his letter to the Galatians, wrote that 'there is neither Jew nor Greek, slave nor free, male nor female, for you are all one in Christ Jesus' (Galatians 3:28). His goal wasn't to obliterate these distinctives but rather to grow communities that thrived because of them. The church modeling diversity in harmony serves as a prophetic sign to our society. As it finds ways of creating, building and connecting truly diverse communities rather than mirroring a society divided by race, creed, age, income, gender and the rest, it announces the kingdom of God is here.

LEADERSHIP

Taking diversity seriously has serious implications for leadership. In a diverse group, top-down leadership can go only so far. Diversity requires bottom-up initiatives that bubble up from the ground—initiatives that are organic and give tangible expression to the full breadth of tribes that make up a church. It takes strong and secure leaders to recognise, encourage and enable this rather than to attempt to fight it and control it. An insecure church leader needs to maintain control—which means diversity becomes a problem. The insecure leader will see diversity as a threat rather than an opportunity because he regards it as undermining his own position, an attack on his role and his responsibility.

MISSION

Diversity is one of the key principles of effective mission in our twenty-first-century, multicultural world. In the Great Commission, Jesus commands his followers to 'go and make disciples of all nations, baptizing them in the name of the Father and of the Son and of the Holy Spirit, and teaching them to obey everything I have commanded you' (Matthew 28:19–20). The Greek word we have translated as 'nations' (*ethnos*) more literally meant ethnic, tribal or cultural groups (see chapter 1). However, our contemporary problem is that we use the term *ethnicity* almost universally to define country of birth. In reality, ethnicity or culture is wider than that.

The Willowbank Report (from the Lausanne Commission for World Evangelism) defines culture as 'an integrated system of beliefs, values, customs and institutions which bind a society together and give it a sense of identity, dignity, security and continuity'. Bikers, golfers, runners, musicians, skaters, walkers, bird watchers, train spotters, painters, poets, clubbers, potters, singers, dressmakers, gardeners are modern-day tribes. We think differently, we see things differently, we learn differently, we respond differently. We are different.

All this inevitably means that to reach diverse people groups we need diverse forms of mission and, therefore, church. Diversity dictates that a one-size-fits-all approach to mission will be fruitless. Intelligent churches understand this. The secret to a diverse mission strategy is to ensure that we identify and understand the needs and aspirations of our communities and then seek to engage with them in their language, their culture and their learning style.

The New Testament clearly distinguishes between *proselytism* and *conversion*. Prior to the coming of Christ, the Jewish people had a well-established process through which devout and God-seeking Gentiles could be admitted to the religion and community of Israel. In this way they were, as Andrew Walls put it, 'effectively decultured as Gentiles' and received into the faith as proselytes—'to all outward appearances they became Jewish'.

The early church obviously understood this model but chose to abandon it in favour of a new approach involving conversion. This clear break with Jewish tradition led to a situation in which Gentile converts to Christ were left to find a Christian lifestyle of their own within Hellenistic society under the guidance of the Holy Spirit. Christian converts, in contrast to Jewish proselytes, were not to be extracted from their culture; instead they were specifically called to remain within Greek society and to develop a pattern of discipleship within that context.

Andrew Walls continues:

> It was their task to convert their society; convert it in the sense that they had to learn to keep turning their ways of thinking and doing things—which, of course, were Greek ways of thinking and doing things—toward Christ, opening them up to his influence. In this way, a truly Greek, truly Hellenistic type of Christianity was able to emerge.

This was a paradigm shift. The Jewish model of the expansion of the religious community—proselytizing—was replaced by a new model of mission—conversion. According to David Smith in his book *Mission After Christendom*:

> The former practice sought to guarantee that new adherents adopted the patterns of belief and behaviour already established as normative within the believing community and to this end they were circumcised, immersed in water and systematically instructed in the Law of Moses.... But when, following the outpouring of the Holy Spirit on his Gentile hearers, the Apostle Peter proceeds immediately to baptize Gentiles as believers in Jesus, he deliberately bypasses the normal cultural barriers thrown up to preserve the internal purity of the covenant community

and accepts Cornelius and his friends as Roman followers of Jesus of Nazareth.

The message is clear—conversion involves not an abandoning of previous cultural identity but rather a turning toward Jesus Christ from inside it. The implications for every intelligent church are enormous. In practice, churches have usually employed the language of conversion while actually requiring people from other cultures and religions to become proselytes. Peter's innovation in refusing to impose on converts more than the central demands of Christian discipleship has rarely been imitated.

Like the Judaizers in the New Testament, the church has often imposed on its converts prepackaged forms of church life, structure and discipleship that have had the effect of extracting them from their own communities and isolating them in such a way as to make it near impossible to witness to Christ from the inside of their cultures. Instead of making disciples of Christ we've made clones of ourselves.

When Peter returned to Jerusalem from his time with Cornelius he found himself at the centre of a huge controversy and the object of much suspicion and severe criticism. The Jewish Christians wanted to guard the very boundaries that he had just ignored in order to step up a Gentile congregation.

Peter's experience has been repeated throughout the history of cross-cultural evangelism and mission. The church's pioneers have usually faced misunderstanding, criticism and serious opposition. Like Peter and generations of pioneering missionaries that followed him, those who build churches beyond the mainstream cultural norms are likely to be accused of unorthodoxy or even heresy. 'Those who have broken new ground for the sake of Christ have found themselves carpeted by the guardians of orthodox faith,' writes David Smith. But he concludes, 'The very survival of Christianity in Europe and

America depends upon the emergence of men and women able to think new thoughts and devise new strategies at the real frontiers of mission today.'

An intelligent church is a diverse church.

YES, BUT HOW?

The truth is that diversity is problematic for everyone. It is difficult. It is messy. A church that draws its members from a single homogenous group is likely to have less stress when it comes to everything from choosing songs to choosing leaders.

While homogeny is useful for groups within churches (for example, young people's groups and young parents' groups), these should always be part of a multifaceted approach to making church diverse. An intelligent church makes room for these different groups not only to engage in mission with those like them but also to meet together and learn from one another. A truly diverse church recognises that it is strengthened, enriched and made more like Christ through having many different sorts of people and traditions in it.

○   ○   ○

QUESTIONS

1. Allow people to be different. Explore different small group models, encourage different worship styles, experiment with different teaching styles. Send a clear message that people do not have to become the same in order to belong.

2. Take a look at the diversity of the community, and work out whether or not the church community reflects that diversity. If it does not, begin to ask why that is and figure out how to overcome the divide. Seek the help of other organisations that can enable this.

3. Take a slot in meetings to highlight different people and their roles. Make sure you celebrate what they do in all of their lives, not just what they do in the church building.

4. Teach diversity as a biblical model of Christianity. Invite people from traditions other than your own to speak or take part in the life of your church. Release your people to take part in joint acts of worship and celebration.

5. As a church leader, become part of a fraternity that goes beyond your comfort zone and seek to learn from others.

CHAPTER 10

DEPENDENT
CHURCH

An intelligent church is a dependent church. Dependency is relying on others to meet needs that you can't, or feel you can't, meet by yourself. It is the act or attitude of relying on someone or something else for support and sustenance. An infant is almost totally dependent, but even in adult life (though we grow into a far greater level of independence) it is both natural and normal to continue to rely on the support of others. Perhaps one of the reasons why Bill Withers' hit song 'Lean on Me', first recorded in 1972, has become such an multigenerational classic is exactly because it articulates this truth so clearly.

A few years ago I found myself going through a particularly difficult period. I felt besieged on all fronts. I was presented with huge opportunities—chief among them the development of Church.co.uk, Waterloo—but at the same time big challenges, not to mention a number of very real threats. It seemed as though everything depended on me, and my ability to keep going and deliver the goods against overwhelming odds. In the middle of this I found myself speaking at a large conference for several days, where once again I seemed to be surrounded by a sea of people with endless requests which I felt

I had to somehow meet. One morning, when I had reached a point of utter desperation about just how much more of this I could cope with, a young girl and her mum pushed up to me in a crowd. They pressed a piece of paper into my hand and hurried away.

I finally found my way back to my room and sat down exhausted. For the first time I looked at the paper. On it was a child's picture of a flower and the sun. The words 'Be still and know that I am God' were emblazoned in bold, coloured ink right across the page along with a greeting which read 'To Steve Love Emily'. I still have that drawing. It still speaks to me. I keep it on my desk. In fact, I'm looking at it right now as I write these words. Time after time over these last few years, often feeling as though I am caught in the fury of a storm, in the quietness I've sat in my study, read those words again and found peace once more—knowing that in all the struggles and battles life brings, ultimately God calls me to depend on him rather than my own resources.

DEPENDENCY AMID COMPETENCY

'Authentic Christianity is not learning a set of doctrines and then stepping into cadence with people all marching the same way. It is not simply humanitarian service to the less fortunate. It is a walk, a supernatural walk with a living, dynamic, communicating God. Thus the heart and soul of the Christian life is learning to hear God's voice and developing the courage to do what he tells us to do,' writes Bill Hybels. It is no accident that Jesus teaches us to address the creator of the universe as 'our Father'.

Earlier in this book I have argued that an intelligent church must be a purposeful church. An intelligent church must plan its activity in a thought-through and thorough way, not only by creating, but also by constantly monitoring, revising and updating its goals and objectives. Not to do so is to fail to take our responsibility to reflect God and his mission seriously.

However, if an intelligent church is committed to competency, its life must also reflect a spirit of dependency. As Zechariah 4:6 puts it success is "'Not by might nor by power, but by my Spirit," says the Lord.' If our mission, planning, activism or public service becomes detached from a dependency on God, it will ultimately prove bankrupt of transformational power and energy. 'The word integrity indicates wholeness,' wrote Mike Riddell, 'and to achieve it requires a harmony between the public and private life. That which we claim to be aware of in our souls must become visible before it is credible. Likewise, our actions need to spring from the depths of our spirit if they are to be of substance and significance.'

Whenever the connection between our mission and a sense of genuine dependency on God is broken, our work becomes impotent and sterile and the light that should be shining in the darkness is extinguished. Our dependence on God, our love for him, and our desire to discover what he is up to and join him is the source of our action; it is our engine, our inspiration and our motivation. The ability to love our neighbour as ourselves is funded by a loving, dependency on and intimacy with God.

THE DEPENDENCY OF PRAYER

I'm a natural activist. However, I have learnt this: service is, in and of itself, a wonderful means of discovering and developing a dependency on God. Several years ago I heard Jackie Pullinger, the well known Christian who works in Hong Kong's notorious walled city amongst prostitutes and drug addicts, speaking at a conference. 'I hear people crying out to the Lord, "More Lord. Give me more Lord. I need more Lord." But I know what their problem is: they are all on the wrong diet.'

Genuine Christian faith, faith that works, faith that gets involved, always leads to a heightened sense of dependency on, and therefore a new intimacy with, God. But likewise faith that is intimate, faith that is an expression of real dependence

on God gets involved and takes risks. Christians have tended to
divide themselves into two groups by temperament. Some of
us are naturally contemplative and want to emphasise intimacy
with and dependence on God while others are more activist
and are focused on 'involvement in community'; some cham-
pion prayer and listening to God while others campaign for
engagement and action; some preach 'wait on the Lord' while
others retort 'but let's get on with it'. However, this dichotomy
is a false one. While the New Testament urges us to keep our
eyes fixed on Jesus, it never does so at the expense of real
engagement in the 'here and now'. Prayer and engagement not
only go together — they fuel and sustain one another. As one of
my friends, Phil Wall, puts it, we are all called to be 'contemplative activists'. Or as Steve McVey wrote: 'There is an awakening
amongst many believers today who are no longer satisfied with
the hustle and bustle generally known as the Christian life.
Call it the deeper life, the contemplative life, or whatever you
will. By any name this quality of Christian life is conceived in
divine intimacy and born in quiet moments spent between two
lovers. Many Christians who are dissatisfied with the emptiness
of the noise are hearing his gentle call to something deeper,
richer.' But why is this dependency, this reliance on God so
vital? Because without it we are lost; lost not just in the sense
that we cannot reflect God unless we know him intimately, but
lost because of the nature of the task that confronts us.

Jesus taught his disciples to pray: 'Our Father ... your kingdom come. Your will be done on earth as it is in heaven.' And,
in doing so made his recognition of the fact that we live in a
world where God's will is not presently done 'as it is in heaven'
abundantly clear. One only has to consider the grinding issues
of homelessness, of abuse, of violence, of war, of discrimination,
of neglect, of famine and poverty to begin to understand this.
But, if God's will is not universally experienced on earth, who
else's hand is at work?

THE REBELLION

The Old Testament tells us little about Satan—he is only specifically mentioned on three occasions. (1 Chronicles 21:1, Job 1–2, Zechariah 3:1). But, the New Testament is very different. In fact, the picture of spiritual conflict it paints can only be fully understood in terms of the unfolding drama between two kingdoms: that of God and that of Satan.

As American church leader and scholar, Gregory Boyd points out,

> Jesus' teachings were not first and foremost about high ethical ideals or profound religious insights, though they are frequently that as well. Rather, most fundamentally they are about what Jesus himself was most fundamentally about: engaging in mortal combat with the enemy of all that is godly, good and true. In his teachings we find many valuable insights into the nature of the war that ravages the earth, insights that should influence our understanding of the problem of evil.

The New Testament presents us with a world under Satan's dominion. Jesus is 'tempted by the devil' (Luke 4:1–13). He heals a woman 'whom Satan has kept bound for eighteen long years' (Luke 13:16), and is finally betrayed after Satan enters into Judas (Luke 22:3). In John's gospel, Jesus often speaks of Satan as 'the prince of this world' (John 12:31,14:30, 16:11), whom he describes as a 'murderer' and 'the father of lies' (John 8:44). He believes himself to be in the forefront of a gigantic spiritual battle: 'How can anyone enter a strong man's house and carry off his possessions unless he first ties up the strong man?' (Matthew 12:29). But, it is his death that Jesus regards as the means of delivering the decisive victory through which Satan will be defeated. 'Now is the time for judgement on this world; now the prince of this world will be driven out. But I, when I am lifted up from the earth, will draw all people to myself' (John 12:31–32).

And according to the apostle Paul, who picks up on this same theme: 'having disarmed the powers and authorities, [Jesus] made a public spectacle of them, triumphing over them by the cross' (Colossians 2:15). Peter adds that Jesus 'has gone into heaven and is at God's right hand—with angels, authorities and powers in submission to him' (1 Peter 3:22). and 1 John 3:8 declares 'The reason the Son of God appeared was to destroy the devil's work.' The New Testament writers are agreed—Christ's victory over Satan is decisive; the war has been won. The powers have been trodden under foot by Jesus.

But, though the cross of Christ may have been the decisive campaign in the war, and assured its final outcome, still skirmishes go on. There are battles still to fight. Once again the apostle Paul makes this absolutely clear. The church's present and ongoing 'struggle is not against flesh and blood, but against the rulers, against the authorities, against the powers of this dark world and against the spiritual forces of evil in the heavenly realms' (Ephesians 6:12). It is because of this that he warns his readers to 'put on the full armour of God so that you can take your stand against the devil's schemes' (Ephesians 6:11). God is somehow still engaged in a battle with the forces of evil, whose greatest desire is to undermine his will. 'Christianity is the story of how the rightful king has landed, you might say landed in disguise, and is calling us all to take part in a great campaign of sabotage' writes C. S. Lewis.

Harry Boer served four years as a chaplain during World War II and spent the final days of that war among marines in the Pacific Theatre. 'The Second Division saw much action, with great losses,' he writes. 'Yet I never met an enlisted man or an officer who doubted for a moment the outcome of the war. Nor did I ever meet a marine who asked why, if victory was so sure, we couldn't have it immediately. It was just a question of slogging through till the enemy gave up.' In Lewis's words, 'This universe is at war. But it ... is a civil war, a rebellion, in that we are living in a part of the universe occupied by the rebel.'

However, an important question remains: When the apostle Paul speaks of our battle not being 'against flesh and blood, but against the rulers, against the authorities, against the powers of this dark world and against the spiritual forces of evil in the heavenly realms', what does he mean? Who are the 'rulers' and 'powers of this dark world'? Who are the 'spiritual forces in the heavenly realms'? Who is it we are struggling against and how do we wage that war?

Some Christian thinkers have argued that, for Paul, the 'powers' and 'authorities' are simply the 'structures of earthly existence'. When the 'spirituality' of human governments, regimes, traditions, institutions, corporations, organisations, communities and families becomes diseased they become 'demonic'. But other writers have regarded Paul's phraseology as referring literally and exclusively to angels and demons rather than to social or political structures. In my view, however, the most intelligent approach is to recognise that the 'powers' are at one and the same time, visible and invisible; earthly and heavenly; personal and institutional. The New Testament writers use terms like 'principalities', 'powers' and 'thrones' both of human rulers and of the spiritual forces which lie behind them. Without the reality of the demonic it is difficult to understand how it is that earthly structures become tyrannical, but conversely, it is equally difficult to grasp how Satan and his angels exercise their strangle hold if not through fallen human structures.

The circumstances around Jesus' death vividly illustrate this interplay. At a human level it was a powerful coalition of organised religion, Roman and Jewish politics, and popular opinion (which was easily manoeuvred and manipulated by the more unscrupulous), which worked to bring Jesus down. But behind all this Satan and his hordes lurked as they orchestrated, distorted and used the human structures of the day for their own evil ends. An intelligent church will take the socio-political nature of evil seriously without ever minimising its individual and personal aspects. Hence we are to fight systemic evil as forcefully as we are to fight individual evil.

It is clear therefore that our task must be carried forward simultaneously on two fronts—through determined prayer and through persuasive action; prayer that expresses and demonstrates our dependency on God and action that demonstrates our commitment to his mission. In the words of Nigel Wright, 'in persuasive action men and women and institutions are called to invest in what is good and true rather than what is false … In prayer the power of the kingdom of God is given access to human life.'

Jesus taught his disciples to pray that God's kingdom will come, and Paul, having reminded the Ephesians that their struggle was against 'rulers … authorities … powers … and … spiritual forces of evil in the heavenly realms', immediately went on to exhort them to 'pray in the Spirit on all occasions with all kinds of prayers and requests'(Ephesians 6:18).

DOES IT MAKE ANY DIFFERENCE?

But the question is often asked, what difference does prayer make? If God is good and knows our needs anyway—why bother to pray? Some Christians have claimed that prayer is primarily for our benefit, not God's. Our prayers do not change God, but become the means by which God changes us. 'When I speak of moving God, I do not mean that God's mind is changed by prayer, or that His disposition or character is changed. But prayer produces such a change in us as renders it consistent for God to do as it would not be consistent for Him to do otherwise,' explained Charles Finney. John Stott wrote, 'Prayer is not a convenient device for imposing our will upon God, or bending his will to ours, but the prescribed way of subordinating our will to his.'

But while this perspective clearly contains some truth about the gift of prayer, any straightforward reading of Scripture would seem to indicate that the impact of trusting prayer is far more than this. We must obviously always be wary of falling into the belief that, in some way, prayer is about asking God for what we want, and then expecting him to supply it—reducing him to a servant, there simply to do our bidding and grant our desires. However, in one of the most curious incidents in Jesus' ministry he caused a fig tree to wither and die. But, when his disciples asked how it happened, Jesus replied, 'I tell you the truth, if you have faith and do not doubt, not only can you do what was done to the fig tree, but also you can say to this mountain, "Go, throw yourself into the sea," and it will be done. If you believe, you will receive whatever you ask for in prayer' (Matthew 21:21–22). And James echoes a similar message: 'The prayer offered in faith will make the sick person well; the Lord will raise him up' (James 5:15).

The belief that prayer makes a difference and significantly influences the outcome of events is central to the Bible—both the Old and New Testaments. Scripture is full of examples of God's faithfulness in responding to the prayers of his people. For example, there are many instances where the Bible directly states that God intended to bring judgement on people or a city but reversed his course of action in the light of prayer (e.g., Exodus 32:14; Numbers 11:1–2; 14:12–20; 16:20–35; Deuteronomy 9:13–14, 18–20, 25; 2 Samuel 24:17–25; 1 Kings 21:27–29; 2 Chronicles 12:5–8; Jeremiah 26:19). In fact, one of the most fundamental assumptions running throughout Scripture is that 'the prayer of the righteous is powerful and effective' (James 5:16).

Jesus frequently taught on the importance of prayer. He repeatedly instructed his disciples to ask God for what they wanted, promising that it will be given to them (Matthew 7:7,11; 18:19–20; John14:13–16; 15:7,16; 16:23). And he encouraged them to pray with persistence — not taking no for an answer (Luke 11:5 – 13; 18:1 – 8). None of this teaching makes any sense if prayer does not actually change things and cause God to bring about a state of affairs that otherwise would not have occurred. In fact, unless it does it is difficult, if not impossible, to explain the urgency that the Bible attributes to the need for intercession and an attitude of dependency on God and trust in his intervention.

'God has of his own motion placed himself under the law of prayer, and has obligated himself to answer the prayers of men. He has ordained prayer as a means whereby he will do things through men as they pray, which he would not otherwise do. If prayer puts God to work on earth, then, by the same token, prayerlessness rules God out of the world's affairs, and prevents him from working. The driving power, the conquering force in God's cause is God himself. "Call on me and I will answer thee and show thee great and mighty things which thou knowest not," is God's challenge to prayer. Prayer puts God in full force into God's work' claims E.M. Bounds.

Or as Gregory Boyd explains, 'Unless it is sometimes true that God brings about the course of events in a way that he would not had he not been asked, petitionary prayer is idle: just as it would be idle for a boy to ask his father for a specific birthday present if the father has made up his mind what to give irrespective of what the boy asks.'

WAYS OF PRAYING

In the history of the Christian church, there are almost as many ways of praying as there are Christians to pray. Means and methods of prayer vary from culture to culture and from century to century. But there is a pattern that emerges from the study of prayer that cannot be denied: it is those who make prayer a priority who most find themselves embraced by an answering God. So Gerard Kelly writes, 'As we pray, our

knowledge of God deepens; we learn to recognise his voice
and to discern his will; we begin to see our own circumstances
from his perspective. Whatever style and system we adopt in
prayer, there is a rule so basic that our faith would not exist
without it — those who make prayer a personal priority will
come to know God more fully than those who pray begrudg-
ingly, fulfilling a reluctant duty.'

Once we understand that we are on a battle field — where
God's will is sometimes thwarted but where Jesus calls us to
pray and work in order that one day it will be done 'as it is in
heaven'; once we understand that we, as soldiers of the cross,
are called to 'put on the full armour of God so that [we] can
take [our] stand against the devil's schemes' (Ephesians 6:11);
then our prayers will sustain our relationship with God; they
will shape us to be more like him — to understand more of
his will and purposes — but we will be ready for hardship, set
backs and disappointments. 'Therefore put on the full armour
of God, so that when the day of evil comes, you may be able
to stand your ground, and after you have done everything, to
stand' (Ephesians 6:13). It is through dependence on God that
we engage in the battle and it is through that same dependence
that we will ultimately triumph.

Writing to the church in Rome Paul encourages his friends:
'Who shall separate us from the love of Christ? Shall trouble
or hardship or persecution or famine or nakedness or danger
or sword?... For I am convinced that neither death nor life,
neither angels nor demons, neither the present nor the future,
nor any powers, neither height nor depth, nor anything else in
all creation, will be able to separate us from the love of God
that is in Christ Jesus our Lord' (Romans 8:35, 38–39).

So, while Paul clearly teaches that we are to 'pray in the Spirit
on all occasions', he obviously assumes that 'trouble ... hardship
... persecution ... famine ... nakedness ... danger ... sword ...
[and] death' not only can, but do happen to Christians. Thus his

encouragement for the Romans is not that these things cannot, or will not, happen to them but that even when they do happen they cannot separate them from the love of Christ. Or, as Gregory Boyd puts it, 'We pray for protection and believe that prayer is "powerful and effective" (James 5:16), but we still lock our doors at night.' Or, in the words of A. W. Pink, 'prayer is not so much an act as it is an attitude — an attitude of dependency, dependency upon God.'

An intelligent church is a dependent church.

YES, BUT HOW?

Perhaps the greatest fruit of a deeper dependency on God is that we slowly find our fears diminishing. The Bible records the command 'Fear not' on seventy-nine different occasions. One of the outcomes of deeper prayer is that we are less prone to panic: our response to pressure is no longer as distorted by fear. As Gerard Kelly puts it, 'The opposite of fear, which is not courage but *trust*, becomes our foundation.' And this growing trust in, or dependency on, God brings to us 'the strength and security; the depth and discipline to face life's pressures when at the centre of our being we have learned to draw on the resources of God's presence.' When we know intimacy with God in the inner sanctuary of the soul, we will know confidence with God in the outer battles of our world.

○ ○ ○

QUESTIONS

1. Take some time as a church to consider where you sit in the spectrum between contemplation and action — are you as a church more likely to be found in a prayer meeting or on a retreat or in a soup kitchen or hospital? If you find that you have focussed too heavily on one aspect of your spirituality, what steps can you take to enhance the areas you have neglected?

2. In what ways does your church demonstrate and develop a sense of its dependence on God? If the work of your church were externally audited, what evidence would the auditor find of spirituality in your community service?

3. Get the leadership team of your church together to answer this question: What styles and systems of prayer have been most helpful in the corporate life of your congregations and/or cell groups? What can you do to enhance the depth and effectiveness of these?

CHAPTER 11

TRANSFORMING
CHURCH

An intelligent church is a transforming church. As Charles Spurgeon said, 'A little faith will get you to heaven, but great faith will bring heaven to earth.' Unless each local church offers and demonstrates the message of Christ that is genuinely life changing—and by extension community and world changing—it has ceased to be a church. It has been robbed of its DNA. It has reneged on the central charge with which we were commissioned by our founder.

We have been made to relate to God and to each other. The recovery and restoration of relationships with God and each other are, therefore, central to the work of God and the task of his church in the world.

GOD REDEEMS

Jesus called his first followers to life-transforming relationships with God the Father and with other people. It is our privilege and responsibility both to model those relationships and to welcome others into them. God is always working to redeem. Just as an artist never uses an eraser but rather works the stray line back into the drawing, so God's purpose is to make all things new—both at an individual and a systemic level.

An old story is told about a preacher who stood talking to a crowd at London's famous Hyde Park Corner on a sunny Sunday afternoon. As he did so a young member of the crowd started to heckle him. He pointed to a shabbily dressed man sitting under a nearby tree and shouted, 'Socialism can give that man a new suit and change what he has! What can your Christianity do?'

The preacher gently replied, 'Your politics can put a new suit on that man, but only Christ can put a new man in that suit.'

Individual change is impossible without spiritual renewal. That is exactly the claim of Jesus Christ: 'I am the living bread that came down from heaven. If anyone eats of this bread, he will live forever' (John 6:51), and 'Whoever drinks the water I give him will never thirst. Indeed, the water I give him will become in him a spring of water welling up to eternal life' (John 4:14). The Christian faith is built around the claim of Jesus Christ to hold the power to feed hungry souls, to refresh life's weary travellers and to bring hope, change and transformation both to individuals and to communities.

Transforming mission knows that solutions never flow from the outside in. They flow from the inside out. Only Christianity can put new people in suits. Only God can see communities truly changed—life by life and street by street. Not only can he do it; he is doing it. Right now.

GOD IS LOVE

The New Testament makes explicit the greatest truth ever fathomed by humankind, the truth that runs throughout Scripture and throughout time: God is love (1 John 4:8). It was this love that first provided the impetus for creation and then for the redemption of that creation through Jesus' life, work, death and resurrection. Love is the foundation of the character of God and is the motivation for all that he has done.

Throughout his life Jesus demonstrated God's extraordinary love but never cajoled or forced people into following him. He simply offered the simple but direct invitation to all whom he met—'Follow me.' The reason, of course, why Christ did not bully or push people into following him is simply this: God is love. Love woos; it does not rape. Love beckons; it does not intimidate. Love does not bully; it cannot bully.

I have a friend who got divorced a number of years ago. Her marriage had lasted only five years and had been from beginning to end a deeply unhappy time. The main reason for this was that her husband was an intolerant man. As far as he was concerned, she could never do anything right. He would shout and scream if anything was out of place in the house, if his shirts were not perfectly ironed, if he noticed a cobweb in the corner of the room, if his dinner was not served on time. He would threaten to leave her if she didn't keep both the house and herself looking just right. She lived in constant fear of his criticism. Her life was made miserable by his constant bullying, and eventually she had to walk away from the relationship.

About eighteen months later she met a new man. They started spending time together and eventually decided to marry. I saw her a couple of years into her new marriage, and she was an entirely different person. She was brimming with confidence, looking fantastic and smiling from ear to ear. I could hardly believe the transformation—and I complimented her on it. She told me that her new marriage was wonderful, that her husband made her feel safe, loved and more alive than she'd ever felt possible. He never bullied her or threatened her. 'The funny thing is,' she observed, 'I'm doing most of the same chores that I did in my first marriage. I still cook the meals, do most of the housework, iron my husband's shirts.' The difference was that she wanted to do all this to please him rather than to avoid his displeasure. He loved her for who she was and not what she did—and that made her want to do good things for him.

Bullying doesn't work, but love does. Love is the greatest power in the universe. It is not coercive. It invites and inspires engagement, response and transformation. God is love and calls his church to demonstrate the same transforming power. Each and every person on the face of the earth is created in God's image and is of infinite worth. Nobody is beyond the pale of God's love.

The extraordinary thing about the Christian gospel of redemption and transformation is that in and through it, God made his move toward us before we trusted him or believed in him. He went first. Paul makes this abundantly clear in Romans 5:8: 'God demonstrates his own love for us in this: While we were still sinners, Christ died for us.' Here is deep truth. People begin to believe in themselves when they know that someone else believes in them. Transformation is never motivated by fear; it is only ever motivated by love. It is only ever a reaction to God's grace, God's initiative and God's love.

LIVES CAN CHANGE

Countless individuals do not believe their lives can change. Whole communities have been forgotten or consigned to the rubbish heap because politicians, sociologists and others have given up. But God never gives up on anyone. The church's job is to help people see that things can change, because God can change people.

Freddie, a thirty-year-old from a rough part of town, who'd spent more than a third of his life as a heroin addict, had no job, no prospects and no hope. To finance his habit, he had turned to crime, earning himself what he jokingly referred to as season tickets for police stations and prison cells. The lowest point came for him one Christmas morning when he woke to find that one of his roommates was staring at him with a sad look in her eyes. As he glanced down, he saw that a needle still stuck in his vein from where he'd shot up the night before. Part of him wanted to change, but he just couldn't see how. Another part of him simply didn't believe that he was worth it.

A chance encounter with a member of a local church put him in touch with a Christian rehabilitation agency, and things began to look brighter. It was their approach, treating him as if he really mattered, that finally triggered a real change. 'To have someone believing in me at that time was amazing—I was totally taken aback by it,' he explained. 'I think once you realise you're worth something, your whole being changes.'

Over a decade ago Oasis Trust set up a drop-in health centre for those who are homeless in London. In the early days I would occasionally work there serving tea and coffee, booking medical appointments, listening to endless stories of joy and pain from men and women who had nothing, who stunk and who were often the worse for drink. I wanted to help them but knew I somehow ended up patronizing them. I had life sorted out—they didn't. I was aware it created a distance between us.

I confessed all this to a wise friend. She said, 'It's simple; when you serve them just look into their eyes and imagine that these are the eyes of Christ. Once you see Jesus in them, you won't be able to patronize them—instead, you will respect them, truly love them.' She was right. Her advice saved me from looking down on them as victims who needed my help and a prepackaged gospel presentation. Ten years on I have seen many of them get cleaned up and give their lives to Christ. I've even had the joy of serving with some of them in Oasis and Church.co.uk.

I realise now that when I first became a minister many years ago I had a fundamental misunderstanding of my role. I thought part of my job was to get people converted. I believed my job was to convince people that they were living empty, meaningless and sinful lives and to get them to pray 'the prayer'. Though I tried to manoeuvre people into becoming Christians by convicting them of their sinning, the terrible frustration was that they didn't very often listen to me. And even when they did, all too often they didn't stay in the faith for very long. It was several years later that I realised the mistake I was making. I was trying to do the Holy Spirit's job, and at the same time neglecting my own. It is God who convicts people, not me. I'm not qualified. My job is simply to love God and love other people and through that commitment reflect his love to them.

CHURCHES TAKE ACTION

God does not transform us as individuals solely for our own benefit. He calls us in turn to become his agents of transformation in our communities. 'This is how we know what love is: Jesus Christ laid down his life for us. And we ought to lay down our lives for our brothers' (1 John 3:16). Much Christian theology has privatized faith, reducing it to little more than a cosy personal choice. However, genuine personal transformation leads us to the recognition that we are to be people who give our lives to bring hope to others and to change the world because Christ gave his to change us.

In 2002 research by the British government into the culture of volunteering in the United Kingdom showed that active Christians were three times more likely than others to be involved with the affairs of their communities beyond their own immediate interests—27 percent, compared to 9 percent. That's good news. The question for the church is what has happened to the other 73 percent?

If we believe that God is able to transform people, then it is our task to ensure we are introducing people to God. When people start to understand that they matter, they start to understand that others matter as well. Every local church, therefore, should be a seedbed of societal change, transformation and engagement.

A few years ago I visited a church with a friend of mine who is not yet a Christian. The church ran an incredible number of projects and programmes for the local community. From healthcare to dance classes—they offered it all. As we drove away from the church, though, my friend turned to me and said, 'That place is incredible! You can learn about anything you like there — well, anything but Jesus.'

The transformational church will not be afraid to wear its faith on its sleeve. Indeed, it will do it naturally and with ease. Authentic Christian faith is always personal but never private. If the truth about God as revealed in the Bible and chiefly through Christ is true, it must be true for all. If it is true for anyone, it must be true for everyone. A christ without universal validity has no resemblance to the Jesus Christ whom the New Testament claims him to be. Christ is Lord of all or none at all. 'Believing the Christian faith means believing that it is true and is therefore public truth, truth for all, truth which all people ought to accept because it is true,' said theologian Lesslie Newbigin.

Rather than retreating into its own privatized world, the church's task is to recover the confidence that the gospel is not simply true for the Christian community but for all communities, at all times and in all places. We believe that every person should have the opportunity of life before death as well as beyond it through Christ.

BE GENTLE

Intelligent transformational mission cannot be bullying and must not impose. The Crusades and the Inquisition (two of the church's darkest periods) both serve to illustrate this point. Genuine transforming faith is never produced by force — imposition only promotes resentment and sometimes even hatred. A dog can always be beaten into submission, but it will be a nervous, defensive and bad-natured animal. However, if it is nurtured and trained with affection and love, it will willingly respond with genuine loyalty and commitment.

'What is unique about the Christian gospel is that those who are called to be its witnesses are committed to the public affirmation that it is true—true for all peoples at all times,' states Newbigin. But, he goes on to add, that those who follow Christ 'are at the same time forbidden to use coercion to enforce it. They are therefore required to be tolerant of denial, [but] not in the agnostic sense in which the word *toleration* is often used.... The toleration which a Christian is required to exercise is not something which must be exercised in spite of his or her belief that the gospel is true, but precisely because of this belief.'

We use the term *tolerance* a great deal in our culture. However, we dilute the term. The dictionary definition of the word *tolerance* is 'the quality of accepting other people's rights to their own opinions, beliefs and actions'. To tolerate is to treat someone with generosity. However, neither of these definitions implies agreement. The only people who can be truly tolerant are those who are confident in what they believe but secure enough in it to leave space for others to choose their own way. To return to Newbigin's words:

> We do not seek to impose our Christian beliefs upon others, but this is not because (as in the liberal view) we recognise that they may be right and we may be wrong. It is because the Christian faith itself, centred in the message of the incarnation, cross and resurrection, forbids the use of any kind of coercive pressure upon others to conform.

I vividly remember a conversation I once had in a pub with some friends. We were trying to find the simplest and shortest definition of love. We went round the table, and each of us presented our own idea. All the usual clichés were offered. However, the winner, it was unanimously agreed, gave a three-word phrase: 'You, not me.' I asked the person who came up with this definition how he came up with it. He pointed us to a verse in which John the Baptist was talking about Christ. The verse reads simply: 'He must become greater; I must become less,' (John 3:30). Love, he said, is all about sacrificing yourself in favour of the other.

This is what Paul wrote of in his letter to the Corinthians:

> If I speak in the tongues of men and of angels, but have not love, I am only a resounding gong or a clanging cymbal. If I have the gift of prophecy and can fathom all mysteries and all knowledge, and if I have a faith that can move mountains, but have not love, I am nothing.
>
> (1 Corinthians 13:1–2)

Our goal is to meet others' needs, regardless of our own. Our evangelistic strategies will always be doomed if we appear to be nothing more than salespeople trying to drag others, kicking and screaming, into the church. Salespeople always have a tough time of it. Why? Because we believe that they will say anything to get our money.

The wonderfully liberating truth is that we don't need to sell God. Imposing Christian faith upon others does not work. It never did work. We don't need to cajole people or try to persuade them that God is good. All we are called to do is demonstrate it. The command we were given is clear: 'Love the Lord your God with all your heart and with all your soul and with all your mind and with all your strength.... Love your neighbor as yourself' (Mark 12:30–31).

Confident faith, secure faith, is relaxed rather than pushy. It is unapologetically passionate about Jesus and his lordship but does not need to, or seek to, take every half opportunity to harangue others about him. Christ will be freely and naturally talked about and seen without having to manipulate or force the subject or the situation. A transforming church is a liberating church for all — Christian and non-Christian alike.

SOCIETAL CHANGE

Societal transformation is dependent on individual transformation. Humanitarianism is never enough. It never has been and never will be. In the end, the deepest poverty isn't just a material problem; it's spiritual at its core. Personal, internal change is an essential ingredient in real social transformation. Throwing money at social deprivation will only ever provide temporary solutions—if that—to the problems confronting our communities and to society. For instance, you can pour endless amounts of money into a poor housing estate struggling with all of the grinding problems of social deprivation. You can rebuild, remodel or renovate its school, healthcare, library, community centre and housing stock. But these changes alone will amount to nothing more than the equivalent of painting over the cracks. A new school building on its own can never raise aspirations, change values or create hope. It will simply provide a very expensive and rather large target for graffiti and stones. If social change and regeneration are your goals, you must seek to transform from the inside out.

That is why Christian faith is so potent. Society will be changed only when people are changed. Sustainable external change is always dependent on internal change. In the words of British Conservative member of Parliament Gary Streeter: 'We are mistaken if we think we can subcontract the social concern and compassion demanded by our faith to the state and simply leave it there. There is a growing recognition that the state can do many things well, but it cannot deliver the personal or spiritual support that we all need to overcome life's greatest adversities.'

An intelligent church is a transforming church.

YES, BUT HOW?

An intelligent approach to transforming mission will always start and end with love for its own sake. It is never a pushy sales pitch but rather an appetizer to the main course of God's transforming love. It is not our job to make anyone believe. Our responsibility is simply to love God and love others. The process is simple. God loves us, we accept that and we love others. God changes us, we accept that and through us he begins to change others. God embraces us, we receive that and we begin to embrace others. God forgives us, we receive that and we begin to forgive others. So it is that God's love and grace work their way into the world through us. Our communities are transformed because, through us, God walks our streets, feels their pain, hears their cries and responds to their need.

○ ○ ○

QUESTIONS

1. To be a transforming church you have to be engaged. Have a think about the issues your community is facing, and plot out a way of getting involved in order to make a real difference. Ask and answer this question: What would the kingdom of God look like in my area, and how can I help bring it about? Try not to use religious language when answering the question. Make sure that your motivation is not to get the church a good name or to build your own profile. Instead check that you are motivated by a love for people and a passion for God. You will probably find a number of areas in which you can get involved, from homelessness to pregnancy crisis. Think through what you are passionate about and what you really want to see change—they are always good places to start. A church can have a communal identity and passion as well—so think that through prayerfully.

2. Think about ways in which your church can encourage and support people rather than browbeat them. Are there judgemental attitudes in the church that hold people back? Do people somehow feel that they don't fit in or can't belong? Are there ways in which you have

excluded or judged people unfairly? Don't allow your-self to be condemned in this. Instead, use the discoveries that you made by working out ways that you can build positively for the future. Are there individuals you can support and encourage, for example?

3. Consider the way your church encourages people to join activities. Do they feel pressured into coming? If so, explore some alternatives to this approach. Make a list of all the people you know who have stopped coming to church over the last year, and then contact them just to let them know that you care. Ask them how you let them down. Don't browbeat them into attending, but commit to showing them the love of Christ. Find simple things that you can do that will help and support them.

4. Make a list of all the activities your church as a whole is involved with during a given month. Ask small groups to list the ministries their members do. Now think about how you would treat the people affected by all of those activities if they were all part of the church. Work out how to make your church a place these people would be glad to visit.

5. Ask everyone in the church to make a list of people they know, and then spend two months focusing on these two questions concerning those people: How would Jesus treat them? What would Jesus say to them? Allow your responses to shape your actions. Do the same thing for your community.

AFTERWORD

○ ○ ○

At the beginning of the fifth century, Augustine of Hippo, arguably the most influential theologian in church history, famously commented, 'The church may be a whore but she is still my mother.' Sixteen centuries later, the frankness of his extraordinary and stark statement still has the power to stun us.

Throughout the ages the church has had countless unloving critics and equally as many uncritical lovers. Historically, neither of these attitudes has served us well, nor will they as we journey forward. Those of us who are committed to intelligent church must imitate Augustine's honesty. We are too deeply committed to the commission Christ gave us to build the kingdom of God—and we love the church too much—to pursue any other course. It is for that reason we must continue to raise our challenge to its unloving critics and its uncritical lovers alike.

An intelligent church is a church whose Christology drives its missiology, which in turn shapes its ecclesiology. All that we believe about God as revealed in Christ (his nature and style) must shape all that we believe about our mission (its nature and style), and the way that we do church should simply be the best way to encapsulate, express and achieve that goal. We must confront the tendency for the process to end up reversed. The shape of the way we do church—our traditions, our meetings, our buildings, our liturgies, our governance, our dress and countless more of our cultural preferences—can no longer be allowed to determine the shape and style of our mission and so limit what our communities and our society as a whole can see or know of Christ. It is time to do church differently.

It is said that William Booth, the founder of the Salvation Army, who was driven by his passion to see God's kingdom come on earth in the here and now, ended his last ever public address, in London's Royal Albert Hall on May 9, 1912, with these words: 'While women weep, as they do now, I'll fight; while little children go hungry, as they do now, I'll fight; while men go to prison, in and out, in and out, as they do now, I'll fight; while there is a drunkard left, while there is a poor lost girl upon the streets, while there remains one dark soul without the light of God, I'll fight. I'll fight to the very end.'

Our Father in heaven,
hallowed be your name,
your kingdom come,
your will be done on earth as it is in heaven.
Give us today our daily bread.
Forgive us our debts,
as we also have forgiven our debtors.
And lead us not into temptation,
but deliver us from the evil one.
For yours is the kingdom,
the power and the glory,
forever and ever.
Amen.

ACKNOWLEDGEMENTS

○ ○ ○

There are a great many people to whom we owe our enduring gratitude for their help in the completion of this project. Special mention must go to Malcolm Duncan, the leader of Faithworks, for his wisdom, insight and helpful comments throughout and especially for his 'yes, but how?' questions. Thanks to Amy Boucher-Pye, Maryl Darko, Bob Hudson, and all at Zondervan for having met our procrastinations, prevarications and postponements with patience, encouragement and love. That these words are in print at all is a miracle of their making. Love unending goes to Cornelia Chalke and Chloe Watkis — they without whom there would seem little point in doing anything much — who have shored up their respective halves of this writing partnership.

Most of all thanks must go to the congregation and staff of Church.co.uk, Waterloo from whom much of this book flows. We may not be intelligent yet, but together we're not quite as stupid as we once were.

—Steve Chalke & Anthony Watkis

ABOUT FAITHWORKS

PURPOSE

The Faithworks Movement exists to see transformation of individuals and communities through Christ. It has three main objectives:

- To inspire, resource and equip individual Christians and every local church to develop its role at the hub of its community, serving unconditionally.
- To challenge and change the public perception of the church by engaging with both media and government.
- To encourage partnership across churches and other groups to avoid unnecessary competition and build collaboration.

The Movement was founded by eleven partner organisations that continue to play an important role in its development. Faithworks has a lead partner in the Oasis Trust, which provides the majority of Faithworks' financial support, gives staff and office space and seeks to provide models of inclusive activity as examples of good practice for the wider Movement.

RESOURCES

Faithworks has made a number of resources available that aim to help individuals, churches and organisations. These include the following:

- *Training and consultancy* help local projects and churches to run professional projects, to be equipped and trained for engagement with the community and wider society and to work effectively in partnership.
- *Published materials* such as books, manuals and guides that help projects deal with the principles and pragmatics of engaging with the community, working with other voluntary and faith groups and working with the government and other statutory bodies.
- *Web-based resources* including a Web site, articles, virtual networks and regular updates on issues such as funding, key opportunities, policy developments and events.
- *Leadership* in helping those involved in the Faithworks Movement to engage with government, media and wider society on issues of social action, social justice and inclusion.
- *Theological reflection* around the issue of the core message and mission of the church.
- *Speakers* for local, regional, national and international events who aim to inspire, challenge and encourage the church to engage with the community unconditionally.

GETTING INVOLVED

There are many ways of getting involved in the Faithworks Movement. Here are just a few:

MEMBERSHIP

Faithworks Membership is free and will ensure you are kept in touch with the Faithworks Movement. Sign up today at www.faithworks.info/join. Membership enables you to access all the resources and information that Faithworks distributes. It also ensures that you are able to connect with people who have the same commitments, passions and struggles as you do. As a member of Faithworks, you become part of a growing movement across the world that is seeking to see radical and lasting change in communities through Christ.

PARTNERSHIP

Formal partnership in the Faithworks Movement is open to all Christian churches, organisations, networks and individuals who sign the Faithworks Charter and Partnership Agreement (for more information go to www.faithworks.info). The Charter sets out commitments and principles for service delivery, and the partnership agreement sets out how partnership in the movement works. There are two levels of Faithworks partnership.

FAITHWORKS AFFILIATES

You can officially affiliate your church, Christian community project or organisation with Faithworks. This is an opportunity to belong to a recognised nationwide network, which will aid your negotiations with statutory agencies and local government as well as increase your funding potential. As a Faithworks affiliate you will receive an official certificate recognising your Faithworks affiliation and the right to use the Faithworks registered logo. In addition to all the benefits of personal membership, you will also have access to free downloads of the growing number of practical tools produced by Faithworks to assist your church, organisation or project in developing effective work in the local community. We also offer affiliate discounts on consultancy and training, and we are constantly reviewing how best we can serve you. To affiliate with Faithworks visit www. faithworks.info.

LOCAL NETWORKS

You can partner with Faithworks as a local network of churches, projects and organisations across a town, county or region. If you are starting a network, we ask you to ensure that the churches and projects that join your network individually affiliate with Faithworks nationally, entitling them to all the benefits of affiliation. However, beyond these simple principles we recognise that each local network will be unique. We therefore actively encourage flexibility in the way local Faithworks networks are established, rather than a one-size-fits-all culture. For more information visit www.faithworks.info. It may be that you are already involved in an effective network. Faithworks is keen to work with and support existing local networks.

As a Faithworks local network, you will be given the opportunity to host Faithworks regional events to inspire and resource your members and beyond. If you choose to operate under the name of Faithworks, your local network will receive a specially designed Faithworks logo, which will include the name of the town, region or area, for use on all literature and publicity that you produce in relation to your Faithworks-affiliated activity.

To find about more about the work of Faithworks, including details contained in this section, please contact:

> Faithworks
> 115 Southwark Bridge Road
> London SE1 0AX
> England
> Tel: +44 207450 9000
> Email: info@faithworks.info
> Web: www.faithworks.info

The Faithworks Charter

Principles for Churches and local Christian agencies committed to
excellence in community work and service provision

O   O   O

Motivated by our Christian faith we

_____   _____

commit ourselves to the following standards as we serve

others in our community work and seek to model trust.

Signed _____

Date _____

Position _____

O   O   O

We will provide an inclusive service
to our community by:

1. Serving and respecting all people regardless of their
   gender, mariwtal status, race, ethnic origin, religion, age,
   sexual orientation or physical and mental capability.

2. Acknowledging the freedom of people of all faiths or
   none both to hold and to express their beliefs and convictions respectfully and freely, within the limits of the law.

3. Never imposing our Christian faith or belief on others.

4. Developing partnerships with other churches, voluntary groups, statutory agencies and local government

wherever appropriate in order to create an effective, integrated service for our clients avoiding unnecessary duplication of resources.

5. Providing and publicising regular consultation and reporting forums to client groups and the wider community regarding the effective development and delivery of our work and our responsiveness to their actual needs.

○ ○ ○

**We will value all individuals
in a way that is consistent with our
distinctive Christian ethos by:**

1. Creating an environment where clients, volunteers and employees are encouraged and enabled to realise their potential.

2. Assisting our clients, volunteers and employees to take responsibility for their own learning and development, both through formal and informal training opportunities and ongoing assessment.

3. Developing an organisational culture in which individuals learn from any mistakes made and where excellence and innovation are encouraged and rewarded.

4. Promoting the value of a balanced, holistic lifestyle as part of each individual's overall personal development.

5. Abiding by the requirements of employment law in the UK and implementing best employment practices and procedures designed to maintain our distinctive ethos and values.

○ ○ ○

We will develop a
professional approach to management,
practice and funding by:

1. Implementing a management structure, which fosters and encourages participation by staff at all levels in order to facilitate the fulfilment of the project's goals and visions.

2. Setting and reviewing measurable and timed outcomes annually, and regularly to evaluate and monitor our management structure and output, recognising the need for ongoing organisational flexibility, development and good stewardship of resources.

3. Doing all we can to ensure that we are not over-dependent on any one source of funding.

4. Implementing best practice procedures in terms of Health and Safety and Child Protection in order to protect our staff, volunteers and clients.

5. Handling our funding in a transparent and accountable way and to give relevant people from outside our organisation/project reasonable access to our accounts.

○ ○ ○

BIBLIOGRAPHY

O   O   O

INTRODUCTION

The quote from Albert Einstein is as cited by Michael Frost and Alan Hirsch in their book *The Shaping of Things to Come*, (Peabody: Hendrickson, 2003).

1. INTELLIGENT CHURCH

The quote about man's concept of God is traditionally attributed to William Temple.

The quote from Franklin Roosevelt is taken from an address given to the University of Pennsylvania, September 20th 1940.

David Beckham's comment on his son's christening was made in an interview with *OK* magazine in 2001 ahead of the publication of his first autobiography *Beckham: My World*, (London: Hodder & Stoughton, 2001).

The Shawshank Redemption was written and directed by Frank Darabont (1994). The film was based on a novella by Stephen King called 'Rita Hayworth and the Shawshank Redemption' taken from his book *Different Seasons*, (London: Macdonald, 1982).

The statistics on suicide are taken from the World Health Organisation's *World Report on Violence and Health*, (2002).

Paul Tillich's quote is taken from *A History of Christian Thought: From Its Judaic and Hellenistic Origins to Existentialism*, Carl Braaten (ed), (New York: Simon and Schuster, 1968).

The quote from Leonardo Boff comes from his book *Trinity and Society*, trans. Paul Burns (Maryknoll: Orbis, 1998).

The quote about loneliness is traditionally attributed to Mother Teresa.

The Prisoner was created by Patrick McGoohan and George Markstein, produced by Granada Television and was broadcast in the UK between October 1ˢᵗ 1967 and February 4ᵗʰ 1968.

Søren Kierkegaard's writings on geese and on God are available in many editions the world over. Of particular interest are *The Prayers of Kierkegaard*, (Chicago: The University of Chicago Press, 1956) and *Provocations: Spiritual Writings of Kierkegaard*, (Maryknoll: Orbis, 2003).

The Tom Peters quote is taken from his book *The Circle of Innovation: You Can't Shrink Your Way to Greatness*, (London: Coronet, 1998).

Theodore Roosevelt's quote was taken from a speech entitled 'Citizenship in a Republic' delivered at the Sorbonne in Paris on April 23ʳᵈ 1910.

2. INCLUSIVE CHURCH

Michael Lloyd's comments on the incarnation are taken from his book *Café Theology*, (London: Alpha International, 2005).

N. T. Wright's quote about the Temple is from the book *The Challenge of Jesus*, (London: SPCK, 2000).

Maya Angelou has written two autobiographical volumes entitled *I Know Why the Caged Bird Sings*, (1969) and *All God's Children Need Traveling Shoes*, (1986). Her collection of poetry *Just Give Me a Cool Drink of Water 'Fore I Die*, (1971) was nominated for the Pulitzer Prize.

'The Subterranean Shoe Room' was written in Michael Frost and Alan Hirsch *The Shaping of Things to Come*, (Peabody: Hendrickson, 2003).

3. MESSY CHURCH

Homer Simpson's quote on his fears of judgemental churches was delivered in an episode of Matt Groening's *The Simpsons* called 'Homer the Heretic', Season 4 Episode 3 first broadcast October 8ᵗʰ 1992.

St. Augustine's words in this chapter are taken from his work *On the Trinity*.

Derek Tidball's quote on love as the nature of God comes from his book in the Bible Speaks Today series, *The Message of the Cross*, (Leicester: InterVarsity Press, 2001)

The Vincent Donovan quote is taken from his book about his experiences of mission in Africa, *Christianity Rediscovered*, (London: SCM Press, 1982).

4. HONEST CHURCH

Nigel Wright's quote is from *The Radical Evangelical*, (London: SPCK, 1996).

The story of Jesus' return during the Spanish Inquisition is taken from Fyodor Dostoevsky, *The Brothers Karamazov*, translated by Ignat Avsey (Oxford: Oxford University Press, 1994).

The Francis Bacon quote if taken from *The Advancement of Learning* originally published as *The Twoo Bookes of Francis Bacon. Of the proficience and aduancement of Learning, diuine and humane* (London: For Henrie Tomes, 1605).

Philip Yancey's words are taken from *What's So Amazing About Grace*, (Grand Rapids: Zondervan, 1997).

The Robert Davidson quote is from *The Courage to Doubt: exploring an Old Testament theme*, (London: SCM, 1983).

F. F. Bruce's remarks about Thomas are from *The Gospel According to John*, (Grand Rapids: Eerdmans, 1983).

The quote from Paul Tillich is from his book *Dynamics of Faith*, (London: Allen & Unwin, 1957).

The Last Temptation of Christ (1988) was directed by Martin Scorsese from a screenplay written by Paul Schrader. The film was based on the novel by Nikos Kazantzakis, *The Last Temptation*, (London: Faber & Faber, 1975).

The quote from Watchman Nee is taken from his book *The Normal Christian Life*, (London: Victory Press, 1961).

Rudyard Kipling's command to 'trust yourself when all men doubt you' is a line from his classic poem 'If', originally published in his collection of verse *Rewards and Fairies*, (Garden City: Doubleday, Page & Company, 1910).

The quote from Lesslie Newbigin is taken from Lesslie Newbigin, Lamin Sanneh & Jenny Taylor, *Faith and Power: Christianity in Secular Britain*, (Eugene: Wipf & Stock, 2005).

5. PURPOSEFUL CHURCH

The Tom Peters quote is still from his book *The Circle of Innovation: You Can't Shrink Your Way to Greatness*, (London: Coronet, 1998).

Lewis Carol's words are from *Alice's Adventures in Wonderland*, (London: Blackie, 1954).

6. GENEROUS CHURCH

The quote about the image of God is traditionally attributed to Blaise Pascal.

The quote 'man is what he believes' was reputedly uttered by Anton Chekhov.

Søren Kierkegaard's story about the cathedral in Copenhagen is from *Provocations: Spiritual Writings of Kierkegaard*, (Maryknoll: Orbis, 2003).

Leo Tolstoy's quote is from a collection of his writings entitled *The Kingdom of God Is Within You: Christianity and Patriotism Miscellanies*, translated from the original Russian and edited by Leo Wiener, (London: J. M. Dent, 1905).

The quote from H. L. Mencken is taken from his book *Heathen Days: 1890–1936*, (New York: A.A. Knopf, 1968).

Walter Brueggemann's words are taken from *Hopeful Imagination: Prophetic Voices in Exile*, (Philadelphia: Fortress Press, 1986).

Homer Simpson's joy at not going to church was expressed in Matt Groening's *The Simpsons* in an episode called 'Homer the Heretic', Season 4 Episode 3 first broadcast October 8th 1992.

The quote about a group of beggars telling other beggars where to find bread was originally about evangelism. It is traditionally attributed to Charles Spurgeon.

7. VULNERABLE CHURCH

Madeleine L'Engle's words about vulnerability are taken from her book *Walking on Water*, (Tring: Lion, 1982)

The Passion of the Christ (2004) was directed by Mel Gibson from a screenplay by Benedict Fitzgerald and Mel Gibson.

The Lisa Marie Presley quote is from an interview with *Playboy Magazine*, (July 2003). I should point out that I read the quote reproduced in *The Week* although the issue number escapes me.

The quote from Theodore Roethke is a line of a poem entitled 'The Dream' from the anthology *Words for the Wind: the Collected Verse of Theodore Roethke*, (Garden City: Doubleday, 1958).

C. S. Lewis's thoughts are from his book *Mere Christianity*, (London: Fount, 1955).

8. POLITICAL CHURCH

The Desmond Tutu quote is from his book *The Words of Desmond Tutu*, (London: Spire, 1989).

N.T. Wright's views of the political nature of Jesus' ministry are expressed widely in his extensive catalogue; of particular interest, though, is his book *Jesus and the Victory of God*, (London: SPCK, 1996).

Dr Martin Luther King Jr.'s 'I have a dream' speech was delivered on the steps of the Lincoln Memorial, Washington, D.C. as part of the 'March on Washington for Jobs and Freedom' on August 28th 1963.

The Howard Marshal quote is taken from *The Origins of New Testament Christology*, (Leicester: IVP, 1976).

Jim Wallis's quote on politics comes from his book *The Soul of Politics*, (New York: The New Press, 1994).

The quote about reading both the Bible and a newspaper is attributed to Charles Spurgeon although similar sentiments have been expressed by many others, perhaps most notably Karl Barth.

The J. C. Ryle quote is taken from *Practical Religion: being plain papers on the daily duties, experience, dangers, and privileges of professing Christians,* edited and with a foreword by J. I. Packer (New York: T. Crowell, 1959).

9. DIVERSE CHURCH

J. B. S. Haldane's consideration that 'God has an inordinate fondness for beetles' was made in a lecture published in *Journal of the British Interplanetary Society* (1951) volume 10.

G. K. Chesterton's remarks are taken from *Orthodoxy*, (London: Bodley Head, 1957).

The quote 'Had I been present at the creation, I would have given some useful hints for the better ordering of the universe' is traditionally attributed to Alphonso the Wise.

Stanley Grenz's words are from *The Social God and the Relational Self*, (London: Westminster John Knox, 2001).

Michael Lloyd's quote is taken from his book *Café Theology*, (London: Alpha International, 2005).

The Colin Gunton quote is from *The Christian Faith*, (Oxford: Blackwell, 2002).

The quote from Pope Benedict XVI is from Miroslav Volf, *After Our Likeness: The Church as the Image of the Trinity*, (Grand Rapids: Eerdmans, 1998) citing Joseph Ratzinger, *Theologische Prinzipienlehre: Bausteine zur Fundamentaltheologie*, (Munich: Erich Wewel, 1982).

John Donne's words are from 'Meditation XVII' of *Devotions Upon Emergent Occasions.*

Michael Pearn and Rajvinder Kandola's quote is from *Tools for Managing Diversity*, (London: Institute of Personal Development, 1998).

'The Willowbank Report' of the Lausanne Commission for World Evangelism is available online from http://www.lausanne.org/Brix?pageID=14322.

Both of the Andrew Walls quotes are from *The Cross-Cultural Process in Christian History*, (Edinburgh: T & T Clark, 2002).

David Smith's words are taken from his book *Mission After Christendom*, (London: Darton, Longman & Todd, 2003).

10. DEPENDENT CHURCH

The quote from Bill Hybels is from his famous book, *Too Busy Not to Pray: Slowing Down to Be with God*, (Leicester: IVP, 1988).

Mike Riddell's words are from his book *The Sacred Journey: Reflections on a Life Wholly Lived*, (Oxford: Lion Hudson, 2001).

Steve McVey's words are from *The Divine Invitation*, (Montreal: Harvest House, 2002) as cited in Tony Horsfall's, *Rhythms of Grace: Finding Intimacy with God in a Busy Life*, (Eastbourne: Kingsway, 2004).

All of the quotes from Gregory Boyd were taken from *God at War*, (Downers Grove: IVP, 1997), except the words on petitionary prayer which are from *Satan and the Problem of Evil*, (Downers Grove: IVP, 2001) citing Peter Geach, *Providence and Evil*, (Cambridge: Cambridge University Press, 1977).

Harry Boer's words are from 'And a Sword ...', *The Reformed Journal* (December 1984) as cited in Philip Yancey's *Where Is God When It Hurts?*, (Grand Rapids: Zondervan, 1990).

All of the quotes from C. S. Lewis are from his book *Mere Christianity*, (London: Fount, 1955).

Nigel Wright's words are from *The Theology of the Dark Side*, (Carlisle: Paternoster, 2003).

The quote from Charles Finney is taken from *Revival Lectures (Lecture 4)*, (New Jersey: Fleming H. Revell Co., 1993).

John Stott's words are from *The Letters of John*, (Grand Rapids: Eerdmans, 1988).

The E. M. Bounds quote is from *The Weapon of Prayer*, (New Kensington: Whitaker, 1996).

All of Gerard Kelly's words were taken from *Sing the Lord's Song in a Strange Land: Spring Harvest 2005 Study Guide*, (Uckfield: Spring Harvest, 2005).

A. W. Pink's words were taken from *The Sovereignty of God*, (Edinburgh: Banner of Truth, 1961).

11. TRANSFORMING CHURCH

The quote about having faith enough to bring heaven to earth is traditionally attributed to Charles Spurgeon.

All of the quotes from Lesslie Newbigin are taken from Lesslie Newbigin, Lamin Sanneh & Jenny Taylor, *Faith and Power: Christianity in Secular Britain*, (Eugene: Wipf & Stock, 2005).

Gary Streeter's words are from a statement called *Stepping Out in Faith*, the full text can be read online at http://website.lineone.net/~renewing/strenc_p.htm.

AFTERWORD

The quote about the church is traditionally attributed to St. Augustine.

William Booth's words were made in a speech at London's Royal Albert Hall, on May 9, 1912.